On Men and Manhood

Also by Leonard Kriegel

BOOKS WRITTEN
The Long Walk Home
Edmund Wilson
Working Through
Notes for the Two-Dollar Window

BOOKS EDITED
Experiments in Survival (with Edith Henrich)
The Essential Works of the Founding Fathers
Masters of the Short Story (with Abraham H. Lass)
Stories of the American Experience (with Abraham H. Lass)
The Myth of American Manhood

On Men and Manhood

LEONARD KRIEGEL

HAWTHORN BOOKS, INC.
Publishers/NEW YORK
A Howard & Wyndham Company

for
Mark Benjamin Kriegel
and
Eric Bruce Kriegel
who taught me how sons feed fathers and fathers feed sons
as each pursues his inevitable man

"Hemingway's Pain: A Case Study in American Manhood" appeared in a
different version in *Partisan Review* 3, 1977, Volume XLIV.

Library of Congress Catalog Card Number: 79–63621

ISBN: 0–8015–0248–9

1 2 3 4 5 6 7 8 9 10

Designed by Judith Neuman

Contents

Acknowledgments

I THANK THE ROCKEFELLER FOUNDATION for a Humanities Fellowship that provided me with a critical year off from teaching.

In a book that is both a personal meditation about manhood and a continuing debate about its fate in American life, my debts proved to be extensive. My wife, Harriet Kriegel, was as perceptive and sympathetic a critic as I could ask for; my editor, Judith Sachs, gave me that combination of insight and tact that makes a writer grateful; my sons, Mark and Bruce, insisted on their own rush toward manhood as this book was being written. It is a better book, as it has been a better life, for their presence.

I owe a special debt to Rachel Paine, who insisted that I answer her questions; and an equally special one to Earl Rovit, who helped me through a difficult time in the writing of this book. I thank the many men and women who patiently answered my questions and allowed me to enter their lives. Over the years, I have discussed some of the issues in this book with a number of friends and colleagues. I want to thank in particular Irving Alter, Marshall Berman, Anthony Bruno, Nelson Canton, Frank Cavaluzzo, Stanley Feldstein, Earl Frederick, Sam Girgus, Bill Herman, Irving Howe, Karl Malkoff, Jacqueline Paltis, Elizabeth Pochoda, Phil Pochoda, Ed Quinn, Adrienne Rich, David Riesman, Ed Rivera, Jeff

Rubin, Clancy Sigal, Arthur Waldhorn, Margaret Walters, and Arthur Zeiger. One of my greatest debts was to the late Mina Shaughnessy, whose ideas about courage and pain were so close to my own that I am no longer certain of the voice—only the message.

Introduction

LIKE MEN, BOOKS HAVE A WAY of shaping their own lives. When I began this book, my plan was to examine the image of manhood as it had unfolded in the development of American literature. But I quickly discovered that was not the book I wanted to write. It seemed to me too limited to meet my own needs or the needs of our time. In taking a fresh look at what our culture saw in manhood, I discovered that I had to examine the ambiguities and tensions it had created, the strengths that it claimed and the weaknesses it tried to disguise. And I learned that I had to ask myself what men had been in America, what they were today, and what they might yet become. Above all, I learned that I was dealing with the most personal of cultural ideas, and that my book would have to be equally personal because it was about the most personal of conditions.

This book was written during one of the most difficult of times for American men, and it was written because I think that the times promise to become even more difficult for us unless we can look clearly at what we can take from manhood's past. Never before has it been more imperative to examine what we are, what formed us, and what changes we must be prepared to make in the future if the idea of manhood is to survive.

This is not an objective book. It contains no statistics, no graphs, no charts on which the emotional state of manhood is laid out. As an idea, manhood has been a source of strength to me, but it has also been, as it has been for every American man I know, an ambiguous legacy, one that has often threatened to swamp us. When I sat down to write this book, I knew that I had to approach the world of American men, *my* world, with as fresh a vision as I could muster. I wanted to write neither an apology nor a defense. And as I worked, I learned that the qualities I most admired in manhood were still to be found in American men, but that they were often to be found where we had not bothered to look for them before. More old-fashioned and traditional than I suspected when I first approached this project, I also learned that I was receptive enough to take the virtues of manhood wherever I might find them.

Almost a century and a half ago, Emerson wrote, "I believe man has been wronged; he has wronged himself." As I look at my male students, at my sons, at myself and my friends, I find myself echoing Emerson. With him, I believe that men have wronged themselves. The idea of manhood in American life has not been a blind aggression loosed upon the world; rather, it has been, at least at its best, that from which an individual man might take his measure and fight for the kind of presence with which he could live. The rituals and obligations that the pursuit of manhood encompassed were not in themselves evil. For manhood was for many of us an idea that sustained life. With all of its problems and deficiencies, it was certainly what helped me through the most difficult encounter of my own life. It taught me, as I hope it is now teaching my sons, that a man could be human yet forceful, strong yet tender, loving yet self-reliant—and not cease to be a man. Our models may be different today, but I suspect that our need for such lessons remains as strong as ever.

MEN pl of MAN

man-hood /'man,hud, -aan-/ n [ME manhode, fr. man + -hode -hood] 1: the condition of being a human being: human quality or nature (make moral postulates that rest less on his scientific knowledge than on his simple ~ —Weston La Barre) 2: manly qualities: COURAGE, BRAVERY, RESOLUTION (send ~ out of him in fear— G.D. Brown) (society everywhere is in conspiracy against the ~ of every one of its members—R.W. Emerson) 3a: the condition of being an adult male (the thing for which he had striven since ~—Mary K. Hammond) (grew to ~ in a frontier town) b: the condition of being a male as distinguished from a female (has become the symbol of ~, which is socially valued—H. M. Parshley) c: VIRILITY d: male genitalia 4: MEN; esp: the adult males (Ireland's ~ . . . were distributed among the prisons of England—O. S. J. Gogarty) (Britain's strength lies in her own ~, standing on her own shores—M W. Straight) 5: mature status: MATURITY (grew up to ~ under the protection of Great Britain—J. H. Underhill) combat aviation has grown to ~—H. H. Arnold & I. C. Eaker)

—from *Webster's Third New International Dictionary, Unabridged*

Chapter One
On the Beach at Noordwijk

Someone once lauded to him Franz Rosenzweig's courageous tolerance of his total paralysis, and Freud responded "What else can he do?" The same remark can be turned on Freud, as it can on all of us who suffer from illness.

—*Ernest Becker,* The Denial of Death

I

ABOVE THE BEACH AT NOORDWIJK, I push forward on my crutches, push against the salt-splayed North Sea wind, marshalling my determination to fight the wind and the bleak nature it embodies. My two-year-old son pulls at my hand, reminding me of how vulnerable I still am. For even here, in this alien Holland, the past can never be laid to rest: It can only be placated. Not the kind of lesson a thirty-one-year-old American man can afford to ignore. For between a man and his son stands the man's past, the confused struggles and momentary victories of his own coming-of-age. Like all sons, my two-year-old holds his father's past and future rolled into a single storehouse of memory and expectation. And like all American sons, he will eventually be trapped by the ambiguities of his own manhood.

I stare down at him, proud but reflective. In my mind, I shape his future. No matter how much I might try to deny it, I know that I am American enough to want this child to vindicate my life here on earth, to justify even the accident of a childhood attack of polio which has left me with lifeless brace-bound legs. I approach the dimensions which I want him to know. A healthy American father, a hero for a time which mocks heroes, distrusts the heroic—father, husband, lover, teacher, man. An example, a presence. I have come through—and to come through in the twentieth century is a kind of heroism: We Americans can still admire endurance, at least as much as a time grown meretricious with self-consciousness permits. Mark and I stand on the concrete embankment above the beach and stare out at the hammering North Sea surf. For the moment, I feel at peace with the world. Mark's fingers curl around the pinky that juts out from the handle of the crutch I hold in my right hand. The weight of my body comes down on my left hand. I feel significant.

I have acquitted myself well: American man. Not an important fate, but not trivial either. Both the struggles and the ambiguities I have known have made up my own manhood. And yet, the process of claiming one's personal manhood is like this North Sea wind, curling around each of us, enfolding us, isolating the individual against his struggles. Men in America share the testing, the need to prove the individual's capacity. This America of ours is, after all, a country of the mind.

My own testing was a war with the virus that entered my body when I was eleven and might easily have proved terminal. From that event, I now etch a coherent past. I want to bank that past as greedily as a miser hoards his dollars, draw upon it for a sense of self, frame an *I* from it, hammer out my manhood from it. My pride is in having survived as a cripple and man: This two-year-old son holding on to my outstretched pinky is proof enough of that. At least for me he is. In America, men steal their manhood from such tests. A son remains an insurance policy who measures the reality of his father's own emergence.

So I stand here, holding my son's hand, and as if I were standing before a fun-house mirror, my past undulates before me. It reflects triumphs, defeats, anxieties, hesitations, distortions, courage, fear, recklessness. I want to see my future reflected in Mark's eyes, but I see only the horizon stretching toward America. Still, I own this moment as I own my manhood. I have paid the prices demanded of me and will settle for no other category than American man.

Mark lets go of my pinky and pulls away. I watch him waddle toward the incline leading down to the beach without fearing for his safety. He is bright, and he accepts the limits we have imposed on him, just as he accepts my crutches, or the patched and peeling leather jacket I have been wearing with the devotion of an acolyte to his surplice ever since my father gave it to me as a present when I was seventeen. "Be careful!" I call to him. But I know he can take care of himself. A herring seller pushing his cart passes me, his eyes following mine to Mark's tiny form which stands alone. He stops the cart, stirs the brine barrel hanging in front. "He wants to be his own man," the herring seller says to me in Dutch. "A little man on the beach at Noordwijk."

To be his own man. To possess the power of manhood, the self-assurance—this promise had been held out to each of us, to me, to Mark, as it would be held out to his own unborn sons, from the very first squalling cries that announce a man's entrance into this world. A man's character is his fate, says Heraclitus. But an American man's fate is first seen in the way he approaches manhood, the way he moves, loves, provides for others. It is a truth sensed at the heart of his being, the dead center of his manliness. He will be what he demands of himself. What would I teach this son whose arrival had announced a passing in my own life, a turning of the corner in my quest for manhood? How would I tell him what he had to know if he, too, were to be a survivor? How equip him to exist in a culture growing increasingly suspicious of the very idea of manhood, even while it threatened to up the ante of the demands it would make upon him?

He wants to be his own man. Well, there were no sureties. No more for my son than for me. To be your own man in America meant that you learned to trust nothing beyond your own capacity, that you stamped your endurance on the only world you knew. I want to teach my son how to maneuver his way through the false pieties, the dead rituals, in which men enclose themselves. I want to hold on to him and then to cut him loose. I stand on the concrete embankment above the beach at Noordwijk and watch, hesitant but approving, as he creates distance between us.

"Come daddy!" he calls from the beach, the shrill childish voice floating into the wind, so that I am not sure of the words but only of the figure of my son. The herring seller leans across his cart and smiles at me, showing a mouth filled with gold-crowned teeth. "Come daddy!" Mark repeats. I am filled with fresh pride at his boldness. I have been put on earth to feel just this. The herring seller points in Mark's direction. "He wants his father,' he laughs, nodding, as if he were giving me his permission to go to my son.

Images of manhood. Streetcorner cripple, now a father, still sucking on my adolescent dream. I will myself to immense prowess; I move toward my son. I must create my man again. Father this time. Lover, provider, teacher the next. But for now, between myself and my son, a demonstration of the authority of manhood is required. I have won the self I claim. There is nothing I cannot do. At thirty-one, I still expect to conquer. No one can accuse me of being resigned or accepting. A man is the sum total of his resistance and he must prove himself. There is no rest when we struggle for manhood. Not even before our sons. For a son is a witness.

"I'm coming," I call. He stands now about twenty yards into the beach, waiting for me. I walk down the incline that leads from the embankment to the beach. The herring seller disappears, the buildings fronting the embankment evaporate, there is nothing but the wind and the clouds and my son waiting for me on the beach and this incredible power that floods my body. I feel an absolute physical sense of myself—potent, naked, alone, certain. Adolescent illusions hang in the air like ripe pears from the Dutch sky. I snatch at them, approaching my son as I knock the very world apart. Mine is a willing surrender to illusion. The desire fathered by manhood leads to my revolt against reality. *The child is father to the man*, I recall. The child I had been, the child I had fathered. Illusion devouring reality. I follow my son, my visible other self. I am going to pick him up, saddle his legs around my neck. Together, we will run across this foreign beach, an American father with his American son.

Habits and dreams and will pick me up, make me new again. I need nothing, no one, other than this son, this emerging self. I am in the movies, in the books. I am absolutely self-sufficient. For there is nothing else to be given to me other than the prerogative of being an American man. The cripple within dies, and a fierce clarity seizes me. Men choose their moments. And in this particular moment, nothing is left to prove because there is no other man to judge me but myself.

My dream of power is pulled from the very heart of America along with the need not to give in to fate alone. At the age of eleven, a virus severs legs from will. I am forced to fall back upon illusion for the first time. For there is no other way to breathe life into the dream I had inherited by being born a man in America. I drift into what my imagination has absorbed and clear a path for myself. Walk where the road can still be cut, and ignore the surrounding trees.

Still, I had to differentiate between my dreams and the actual conditions in which I existed. The fact remained that I could not run, could not even walk without the braces strapped to my legs and the crutches I gripped. But as I approach my son on the beach at Noordwijk, the braces and crutches disappear. For one hallucinatory moment, I can run again. I believe that literally. For that one moment, I negate the reality of the virus, all the reminders of my *condition*. Aspirations of the uncrippled cripple, ghosts of my own past floating free in Vermeer's sky.

I reach the bottom of the incline. My crutches slice the

sand, sink. I push up on shoulders liberated by the power of myth now, pushing like Moby Dick himself rising from the sea. And then sink, Ahab again. The dream evaporates as suddenly as it has seized me. I can barely walk towards my son, the crutches sink deeper and deeper into the sand with each step I take. I will drown in sand before I reach him. I will die of rage unless I can smash it against something. I caricature illusion now. Nonfather, nonrunner, nonhusband, nonman—the vision has popped, I want to scream.

The wind howls against the beach, chokes off the scream in my throat. Mark's face is pensive with fear, recognition. I feel exposed to his glance, betrayed by his eyes. The manhood game has caught me, tricked me, hurled me to the ground leaving only the murderous rage in my heart. I want to destroy, to prove my presence. But to whom? I will not seek understanding, nor sympathy. Just this need to declare a finish, this murder in the heart. Only the manhood game is never finished.

Mark retreats before the puzzle of this other father. It is evident, even to his two-year-old mind, that he must be his own man now. I can feel the herring seller's eyes stabbing my back. The past breaks loose from its moorings, reality floats free. There was never a man who did not desire to get even.

"Mark go?" my son asks hesitantly. He edges deeper into the beach, away from me. *He wants to be his own man. A little man on the beach at Noordwijk.*

"No. Wait for me." Before I can try again, my wife is suddenly at my side, staring first at our son, then at me, her face puzzled, then overwhelmed by the rage in my eyes. Mark ferrets himself away from me, glancing at her.

I turn, throwing myself out of the sand trap, exaggerating the very difficulties that threaten. "Please!" I hear her insist. "Don't do that to yourself." I ignore the voice. I want to recapture the illusion. I want to run again. In the very calm she wants for me lies the risk of madness. I do not want to surrender to passivity, to acquiesce to reality.

I manage to get back to the incline and move up the embankment, humiliated but still filled with rage. The herring seller is still there, watching. When my eyes meet his, he turns and pushes his cart before him, leaving me to myself and the sharpness of the wind from the North Sea. He has witnessed my failure: I would like to kill him.

II

WHY DOES THAT MEMORY pulsate for me even today with all the pressures and contradictions of being both a man and an American? I still find myself checked by that memory, stopped hard on my way, as if I had left some particle of the man I was on the beach with my son. I inevitably drift back to that scene and go through the process of coupling my American manhood first to illusion, and then to rage. And I wonder, finally, whether this is not the pattern for each of us. I do not want to presume to offer that moment, or any moment of my life, as a paradigm for anyone else's struggles but my own. And yet, that is exactly what I do. I stake a claim for each of us, for each American man. I stand once again before my two-year-old son and discover that the first hurdle is allowing what one loves most in this world to create and then to destroy illusion. A man should be the impresario of his own illusions, and only then, he discovers, will he be able to open himself to the judgement of what he most loves on this earth. A child is one's substance, but a son in America is a judge, the barometer of whether or not a man has measured up. But the burden of that expectation is too great, both for the son and for the father.

Ultimately, mine was the rage of the witness who stands back and sees himself drowning. And what I saw was that everything I had struggled for would be taken from my grasp. I saw the inevitability of what Mark would face in his time, and my rage hardened into permanence.

Even today, I want what I wanted on that beach—to set myself right with my past. To run again, to live out the very fantasies that we know are adolescent, to catch my manhood as it is being formed: an American legacy. I want to re-create my past, to get even with accident, to move into that darkness which harbors my courage and my power and my selfhood and all the other shaman names we give to those qualities we hunger after.

I know that something is missing. I have been tricked, lied to, have given in to illusion. And above all else I have been tested. For the self pressed to its aspirations declares what a man is, and what he can be, here in America. In my resistance to what actually occurred on that beach in Noordwijk, I discover what my dreams of manhood are.

This, then, accounts for the violence of my reaction to what must be considered a minor event. It wasn't that I could not run on the beach with my son. I had long since made a highly successful "adjustment" to what the virus had left. Compensation was easy enough, demanding merely the substitution of one kind of performance for another. No, what had been called into question here was the endurance I had grafted on myself, that virtue I most highly valued. For endurance was critical in the confrontation with the myths that had been bequeathed to me long before I thrust my individual *I* into the American battle.

No American man could afford to be anything less than capable—this was the price of being an American. The world as it was issued its challenge; the American man as he was offered his answer. We lived in the midst of a siege where each man was bound to an isolation that denied the possibility of any solidarity with others, particularly other men. To be both American and man was to be man alone—and to lack even the belief in the *absurd* with which European men had tempered their condition. The self was demanding because it could be nothing else and could turn nowhere else—not even to a philosophy like existentialism, whose very threat of emptiness became a source of comfort.

Isolation in America was man's natural state. To be alone was necessary, perhaps even enviable. There was no other recourse but in one's own living consciousness. As a cripple, I was deeply aware of those boundaries the world had set for me. I would not have been conscious if I failed to grasp them. I knew from the beginning that I would be classified as both pariah and victim, to be pitied, shunned, praised, labelled, and classified. I knew that for as long as I remained alive, I would find myself admired for my "courage," for my "toughness," for my "determination." I knew also that I existed within the peculiar paradox of manhood's American forms: that a man had to learn to accept defeat as irremediable and yet pretend that he was actually asserting his freedom in fighting against such acceptance. To go to your fate was unavoidable; to go quiescently was disgraceful. Expect nothing, but act as if you want everything. You broke the harmony of nature with crutches and prostheses, then employed them with the subtle daring that made them accoutrements of survival. For when the odds against a man's claiming his own existence are great enough, then existence itself could be transformed into defiance. You could seize selfhood from those who insisted on being blind or indifferent to your manhood. My struggle was real—perhaps it was the normal man who had to look over his shoulder, wondering whether or not he was good enough to survive.

"Man is nothing else but what he makes of himself!" cries

Sartre. Even if I were to be defeated, to sink in the sand, I could still carve my manhood out of that agony and doubt. I had at least earned my survival. In the normal's language, I had "overcome my handicap." In my view, he still had to earn *his* survival. And so it was that he would shadow me, always nervous in my presence; so it was he would clothe me in the pious sentimentality of Tiny Tim. Occasionally, however, he would discover that we were brothers under the bone: Each of us would be forced to recognize the man within. We had to see each other. And then I began to wonder whether my manhood was better than his, just because mine had been tested and his had not. The threat of my visibility demands my dismissal; the fact of his presence inspires my contempt. We are even for the moment.

I remember the wind cutting against my face. I no longer want to murder the herring seller, a man who could not understand my rage. After all I am still alive. I sit in the bar, sheltered from the North Sea wind, and stare out at the empty beach. In a world filled with success, I still have to set an example for my son. No disguises, no pretense, just imposing myself on my time. I do not want to serve as inspiration for other men. I am satisfied with this fatherhood, difficult as it is.

"I will set my life upon a cast / And I will stand the hazard of the die." Villain or not, I sympathize with the pain of Shakespeare's Richard. It is a pain absorbed in a defiance that is vital to his crooked nature and to my unsated rage. Richard is human, recognizable—I see myself in him. A man stands up before the measure that has been meted out to him. Richard, too, is an adolescent. Only there is more to the adolescent's desire to prove himself, to call the limit on what he can endure, than mature men are willing to admit. Richard is a model. Spawned by the indifference of accident, he imposes his scars, his unrepentant evil on the world. But just as Shakespeare and the world insist that he acknowledge his evil, Richard insists that they acknowledge his presence. To be a man is to demand an accounting for your life, even when that accounting leads to death.

I wish to match the man within to the challenge outside. Like other American men, I enclose myself within dreams of dominance. Each of us harbors a secret self, a man thrust upon earth to shape it to his will. The world's reality snatches at you, but you respond by seeking a way in which you can exert a solitary pressure for change, gathering momentum from the clear harsh limitations of your own existence. There is something awkward, brittle, about such fantasies. But there is something heroic, something manly about them, too.

III

I STRUGGLE TO MATCH the fantasy with my performance. *Performance* is an embarrassing word; *manhood* is an embarrassing word. Notches on our contemporary belts. It is so much easier to make the idea of manhood humorous. Only to be a man is to commit yourself to the need for performance. No amount of humor can disguise that. A man performs in order to set the terms of his life beyond his limitations. He performs to affirm the idea that accident is a form of opportunity. Mere physical survival may never quite be reward enough for the agony it demands, but it remains, nonetheless, an immense source of pride for those of us who have pulled our survival from the ashes of our being. "Illness is an object," writes Ernest Becker. "We transfer to our own body as if it were a friend on whom we can lean for strength or an enemy who threatens us with danger. At least it makes us feel real and gives us a little purchase on our fate."[1]

My body is a constant reminder of my fate. To have come through is every American man's dream; for me, it is the very integrity of my existence. Every time I take a step, every time I make love, every time I hold my son, I translate death into capacity. Always, performance is central—it would be non-sense to deny that. And I do not hesitate to admit that I want the quality of my performance to be recognized by others. For unless manhood is acknowledged by others, it counts for little.

It would be so easy, I think, to blame *alienation* or *technology* or any of the hundred other modern soporifics for every question. In every age, not just our own, manhood was something that had to be won. Were men in the past any more certain of how to respond to the demands made upon them? I tell myself they were, but how can I know? Our options today are abundant. Why, then, do the choices we make seem forced upon us?

I look at American men and I see the reflection of the cripple's perennial struggle to measure performance when the rules of the game are constantly shifting. One simply must learn to live with the lack of surety. No matter what I did, no matter what the quality of my performance—as father, as teacher, as provider, as lover—what haunted me was the recognition that my triumphs could so easily be seized by others. To what extent is performance the measure? Men deny its validity, but it dominates our consciousness; it bestows the gift of self. The trouble is that none of us is ever quite certain of where performance ends and the parody of that performance begins.

I am comfortable with the need for challenge, the dream of a heroic existence, perhaps more so than other men, simply because I have had to struggle for the trappings of manhood in a world grown increasingly indifferent to it. In the works of Bellow, of Lowell, of Mailer, life is most immediate when it forces the individual into a corner, heightening the possibilities that it opens for him. As if when the trap springs, the man emerges. Manhood demands that each of us defy categorization. We each live with the intimate dread of our own incapacity. We each need to accept the tests of our performance while we learn to deny the legitimacy of those who set the standards.

I knew the tests I gave myself. I knew how consumed with ambition I could actually become, I knew how easily my desire to seek affirmation from a world indifferent to my fate could be broken off, twisted away from its fulfillment. Like most American men, I had learned to behave as if I had created myself: a man alone. And like all American men, I often found myself hounded by hesitation, secret doubts, confusion over what was expected of me. Balanced against these was the need to force myself over whatever obstacles stood in my way. I accepted the necessity of action as I did the limitations declared by the virus. And yet, I could still ask a reckoning of that virus. My difficulty came in controlling reality before it passed into illusion, particularly when I grew tired of the close-in combat, the everyday drudgery of strapping braces to legs and moving out.

No one, I discovered, lived more consistently with the manhood he sought than did the cripple. It was simply impossible for me have come through, to have claimed a self, without accepting the need for courage. How many times did the cripple in me have to place his body next to that which threatened it? Another notch on the belt. Even nature was a field mined with booby traps, an explosion of destructive possibilities, demanding a stealth and measurement disproportionate to what normal men had to muster. You had to learn to accept ice and snow and rain as enemies, you had to walk the streets with eyes alerted to the sidewalk debris, searching for oil slicks or dead leaf clusters or pieces of paper

or patches of sand with the wary potential for imminent encounter of a soldier in a World War II movie scouting a
Pacific atoll.

Such enemies were real, they were intimate. They taught
me that it was possible, as Becker writes, to look at the enemy
within my body as "an *object,* an adversary, something
against which to marshal one's courage; disease and dying
are still *living* processes in which one is engaged."[2] They
taught me that in order to survive, I simply had to be better—
better as performer, better as man. And they fed me a sense of
my own singularity that became the "dirty little secret" of
my life. Of all confessions, this is the most difficult to make: I
came to feel a certain contempt for other men who did not or
could not match my prowess with their own fallibility.

Having lived with pain as a simple cipher, in much the
same manner as a man learns to live with his appetites, how
was I to accommodate myself to a culture in which grown
men rhapsodized over the *courage* of an athlete who earned
his living on aching knees? Only immediacies were entitled to
respect. If we really are nothing else but what we make of
ourselves, then the man who made himself a man also made
legitimate the traditional "masculine" virtues, the very virtues which ultimately became his embarrassment. His needs
could not be analyzed out of existence, not when he gambled
so much of himself to legitimatize those needs.

As long as I was conscious of the pressures on my particular existence, I could claim a place for myself in this world. I
would reverse the concept of *stigmatization* so that it put me
beyond the range of the normal man but did so on terms
which I chose.[3] I would not settle for a drifting lesser normalcy. To be a man was to make demands upon others as
well as upon myself. To be a man was to seek out ways in
which the existence of others was an encounter with my own
ambitions. Invariably, however, the challenges I had to han-

dle were not necessarily those I sought out—they would continually creep up and catch me unawares. Always I would experience that momentary surprise as the element of exposure slipped into consciousness and jabbed some naked nerve. I would lie there, amazed at the intensity of the pain, defenseless. As it is in sex. A momentary release. And then back into consciousness, like a spotlight snapping on my poised body.

IV

SHE GOES TO SHUT THE WINDOW and the man, myself at nineteen, watches the way her naked body moves across the room. I think I am detached. But I am disturbed because I see myself watching her movements. I do not want to expose this stopping and starting, this feeling that I am lying in bed in the midst of a fever, although certainly not sick. While fucking, I square myself with time. I want the bronze medal. I stare at my toes that peep out of a thin sheet. Dead legs of a lover. *For a gimp you performed well.* My mind laughs soundlessly. "Want a drink?" she asks. She opens the blinds to let in streams of afternoon sun. She is naked at the window but oblivious to her body.

"No thank you." I want to say something sharp, quick-witted. Language leaves its mark. She returns to the bed and sits down on the edge, but I say nothing. She reaches across me and takes her cigarettes from the night table. Irritated with her, I narrow my life to questions of purpose. I do not know why I am irritated with this woman, and so I grow irritated with myself. I know what I am going to ask her. What men want to know, whether they ask or not. How do I measure up? It does not matter that my legs do not function;

that is simply an additional challenge. "How was it?" I ask. And hate myself for asking. And hate her for not anticipating, for making it necessary.

Her eyes sweep my prone body. "Join the ranks," she says. "Do you want to be graded?"

I shrug. This woman is all right; she knows more than I do. She is perhaps thirty, older than I am, and that, too, irritates me. Sex is like everything else a man does. The need to be graded. Good, better, best. A grammar for the body.

"Why make it a trial?" she asks. "Why can't pleasure just be?" She puffs on the cigarette. "When I first started, I used to think it was more difficult for us, only it's men who have the curse. Why can't you just have a good time instead of all making it such a contest? God, you must hate each other."

"No," I insist, "it's not hate." I am afraid of saying too much. Women seem self-possessed, competent. I am afraid that she is mocking me. She possesses a distance from herself that I cannot afford. I wonder whether manhood itself is simply a disease, like the other one I know so well. Well, we grow comfortable with our diseases. And the morning comes when you wake to discover that it is even more difficult to live without them than it is to live with them. "It's just. . . ."

"That you have to cast your shadow on some piece of ground," she interrupts. And laughs. "Each of you is always wondering how much of a liar the other is. How much does he know that you don't?"

"About you? About women?" She is a divorcée and I wonder now what her husband was like. It is the first time I have ever thought of him, although this is our third time together.

"About everything. About each other, most of all. Men create virgins and men create studs." She touches my foot. "Can you feel that?"

"I can feel everything," I say quickly.

"I don't know what that's like," she says, as if she were talking to herself, alone in the room.

I wonder whether it is what men have created or what has been created for us. The other side of performance. What begins as pleasure turns in on itself. Still, it was easy enough to brand performance "macho," even then, in 1953. And yet, it is difficult to ignore it, to bury it beneath its strutting artificiality. After all, performance has its specific commitments, and it provides the exhilaration of letting you prove that you remain superior to your circumstances.

Even the gamesmanship with which you manipulate the environment has its place. All right, grade me, lady. Are my hands caressing enough? my tongue quick enough? my cock hard enough? my eyes aware enough? Casanova, Lord Byron, P. T. Barnum, Rusty the Prong, lascivious monks from de Sade, Paul Bunyan—love rides us down into life. How many did you fuck? Incessant buzz buzz buzz on streetcorners all over the nation. A world full of women tones the very impossibility of the thing. The fantasy pulls at our deepest instincts, shapes the future, overwhelms fear with the greater fear of being left behind.

She turns away again and sits with her back to me on the edge of the bed. Suddenly, she seems small, almost childlike, and I wonder why what I do with this woman, with any woman, counts for so much. Why do I have this self-conscious need to reveal no weakness, to translate weakness into strength, to succeed in her eyes? After all, she will never be more than a stranger to me. The necessity of taking risks in pursuit of my own substance irritates me now. All right, and in my mind I say it to her: "Lady, I want more than pleasure. I want a certain standing in your eyes. It is not necessary to be a sexual outlaw to know that much."

Men communicate their fears through their efforts to control sex. She has caught me waiting to be patted on the head and she has kicked me in the balls. I stare at her back and feel the fool. No man ever quite rids himself of the anxiety of performance. I feel it at nineteen, I will feel it forever. Even if I deserve it, I am aware of the shame, the haunting sense of a scene that is to be played over and over again in any man's lifetime. And I cannot even take refuge in "the cripple."

The performance is like the death you grow to anticipate with all its inherent terrors and obligations. But I enjoy it now, play with it. Challenge and response—Darwinian legacies. I do not really believe this enjoyment is unhealthy. It does not leave me uncomfortable, and I do not think it leaves most men uncomfortable. No, it leaves us eager. There is a certain sense of risk in sex. This is, after all, the area in a man's life in which he is most completely exposed, most open and alone, wanting approval from the women who come to weigh his style and pass judgement on the prince or pauper within his heart. Sex was meant to engage a man's energies, direct his strategies, meant to heighten existence itself.

Years have passed, and all the memories seem to fuse into a single vision. I find myself looking back, wondering whether the greatest sin we have left the generations that follow us was making sex, too, a tepid affair. In place of performance, we bequeathed a passive fantasy. After all, a man runs risks with himself only when he does the hard-nosed grubbing that reality demands, only when he is willing to express power and vulnerability in the same gesture. But a fantasy that is never put to the test has neither quality. The gift of passivity, in itself, demands no payment, just as it demands neither physical nor psychological contact. If performance can be branded macho, then fantasy is masturbatory.[4]

V

THE BEACH AT NOORDWIJK haunts me; I search for different openings into the past, for the man working into himself. Space is all around me. It heals. Illusion, I have discovered, can carry you too far. I want a different balance.

It is New Year's Eve and I see myself riding the subway down to the Lower East Side. The party is in an old dimly lit tenement in a neighborhood which will soon be known as the East Village. But this is the night in which 1955 will become 1956 and the neighborhood is still the Lower East Side. The party is in an apartment that is up four steep flights of stairs. I enter the building in the cold darkness. The corners of the narrow hallway dipped in urine, and dried, like a smell from a Bowery shelter. Sweating walls, clotted paint—the poverty is so exaggerated as to seem almost staged. I examine the staircase—the first thing I do whenever I enter a strange building, since each staircase is unpredictable, a new challenge for me, a different threat. This one is sectioned off into three parts, each of six steps, with a landing between, so that a corridor of space, around four feet wide, runs from the roof above the fifth floor to the black-and-white tiled entrance landing on which I am standing.

The stairs are scratched, chipped, the banister of cast iron. It has been painted over a dark forest green which blends to near-black in the dim light provided by the forty-watt bulbs pinned to each landing. I maneuver my way upstairs, pausing to look down at each landing. As I approach the fourth floor, where the party is already under way, I feel as if I am staring down an unused mine shaft. The dim light makes the space below me stretch out, then disappear into shadow so that by the time I reach the apartment landing it is as if I am hundreds of feet above the entrance. I know that it is actually no more than forty feet, but the impression remains, nonetheless.

Hours pass, the year changes, I drink to it. I am with a woman I do not know who tells me that I look like her English lover who died in Korea. I drink, I did not even know the English had been in Korea, I am interested in her, but not interested enough. During the four hours that I remain at the party, I think about the staircase. I am looking forward to descending the staircase and the expectation heightens as the evening goes on. The woman is talkative, intelligent. I think about the angles of descent, about the empty mine shaft plunging to the dimly lit bottom. Going up, the banister was on the left. I will have to descend the stairs backwards. I am afraid. The woman keeps talking. I plan my descent. I will have to hold one crutch in my right hand, brace the other crutch against the banister with my left thumb, and maneuver my legs into the blackness behind me as I seek the solidity of the step below. The weak light will shadow the landings. My mind plays with the potential for disaster. I see my body falling through blank space—I can think of little else. Fear and anticipation mingle, then the fear disappears and there is only anticipation. Like sex. A need for the specific gesture.

Just before 2:00 A.M. I decide to leave. The woman is puzzled; she would like to come with me. I am sober enough to know that I do not want her to. I stand alone at the head of the staircase. In order to gain leverage, I must lift my body by straightening the right arm until all my weight is on the triceps and forearm. Then I shift my weight to my left arm, which pushes up from the banister, while I pin the other crutch against the banister with my thumb. I float in space, lean out and over the banister, so that the body in which I have invested my future moves into the emptiness, four stories above the tiled floor, staring down into the muted distance of the mine shaft, staring into its mouth. My awareness is absolute, clear, my head thickens not with the liquor I have drunk but with the grip of my vanity. No one else on the staircase, either coming or going. Shrouded in the dim light, I seize the moment. Life is immediate, tensile with the immensity of its own promise, as I lean out across the banister into hostile space. Suspended, almost frozen, I meet the virus head on, a spectator at my own performance.

The *only* thing keeping the virus from claiming the rest of me is the power in *my* body, *my* arms, a power I have laboriously built up, doing hundreds of pushups and parallel bar dips each day, soaking my hands in brine to toughen the thick callouses even more, working with weights, springs, coils, dumbbells. Stubborn insistence seizes my mind and tells me that I can now determine the course of my fate. I have captured the man within, have stolen him from the virus, and I want to laugh with the pleasure of it. I am filled with a surge of joy so great that its intensity is frightening, my hand begins to slip down the banister, and then a voice cries out from somewhere inside, "Not now! Don't give it the victory! Be the man you've made!" My fingers cramp, dig hard against the cast iron, hold, until I understand that it is over—I have claimed my body once again. A man must be a man. A man must be better than himself.

VI

ANOTHER SURPRISE CONFRONTATION with my manhood, this one embarrassing for what it reminds me of. That night, I recall, it was still possible to believe. I had a moment in which I felt myself suspended in space, beyond the reach of circumstance, free to choose, to embrace the possibility of death and then to dismiss it as an inadequate alternative. Never again would I fuse my existence with the ability to choose the course of my life. It was through the acceptance of risk, the legacy of accident embodied in the cripple's condition, that I broke through to manhood, hanging four stories above the dingy tiled entrance of an East Side tenement.

Men clutch at manhood to control the anguish and turmoil of their lives. And yet, I knew that I was not a better man for the virus' having slipped into my blood. Suffering can neither dominate nor transform a man's life. But it does create choices, possibilities. And choices, finally, imply acknowledging risks. If you allow yourself to be categorized, you are accepting the ways in which society chooses to eliminate risks, to subdue the realities they impose.

And is not this the very condition that threatens men today? For men have discovered that they have been assigned a variety of new classifications. They are suddenly frozen into a new time, they must be both passive and spontaneous at once—all in the cause of liberating themselves! New times bring new demands, and men now chart the dead ends and blind alleys in which they find themselves trapped. And men discover that *liberation,* too, is only a word, like *courage* and *manliness* and *strength.*

"I want to screw the world now as much as I did then," the forty-five-year-old businessman-turned-dropout says as we nurse our drinks in a Village bar. "They got you coming and going and you're supposed to pretend that it feels good, that you've never felt better in your life. Jesus, this is no world to be a man. Maybe it once was, but it's been dipped in shit since."

He wants something real to struggle against. "Like you," he insists. "Disease is something real." What he means is that he thinks that I have learned the cost, that I understand that only the man who defines himself is capable of meeting that cost. He is not talking about suffering or even about disease. Suffering is rarely more than a question of how much you can take, and he knows that as well as I do. A certain turn of the screw will elicit pain from each of us. No, the source of pride is in having come through, in having managed to transform even disease into a performance.

A man learns to adapt his vulnerability, his pain, to his needs as a man. In his quest for a usable self, a meaningful manhood, he struggles to put his moments to use. I stare at myself on the beach at Noordwijk and I catch the fantasy as it catches me. There is the man I once dreamed of being—and then my body sinks into the sand, my very being buried in the lost vision. But now I am myself once again and I lean across the banister above the tiled floor, aware of the choice before me. If that was the man I once dreamed of being, then here is the man I am yet going to be, the process hard but malleable. Past and future solidify here, are made one. Both demand resistance.

A man has to fight against the power of accident. To face the world as it presents itself, to respond honestly to each new situation—men have been asked to do this from the beginnings of time. "Let a man then know his worth," writes Emerson, "and keep things under his feet." A man's dignity finally consists of the terms of the struggle he declares. To live with that struggle is to be man enough—for himself and for all those sons still waiting on the beach.

FOOTNOTES

1. Ernest Becker, *The Denial of Death* (New York, 1973), p. 144. My debt to Becker is extensive particularly to this book. Few thinkers have handled the problem of coming to terms with the need for the heroic so well.

2. Ibid., p. 104.

3. I have taken the idea of *stigmatization* from Erving Goffman's *Stigma: Notes on the Management of Spoiled Identity* (Englewood Cliffs, N.J., 1963). I have, however, turned Goffman's argument around, since I believe that stigmatization can prove to be liberating through the very distance it provides from the world of the *normals*.

4. Where masturbation had once offered no more than a kind of mechanical satisfaction, it now seems to have become an end in itself, at least if one listens to many of the voices around us. For a sense of how widespread this view of masturbation has apparently grown, the reader should consult Natalie Gittelson's *Dominus: A Woman Looks at Men's Lives* (New York, 1978).

Chapter Two
Manhood and Performance

If the fate of twentieth-century man is to live with death from adolescence to premature senescence, why then the only life-giving answer is to accept the terms of death, to live with death as immediate danger, to divorce oneself from society, to exist without roots, to set out on that uncharted journey into the rebellious imperatives of the self.

—*Norman Mailer,* The White Negro

I

THE SIGN WAS PAINTED on the side of a tenement—red, white, and blue letters absorbed into the dead yellow of the fading brick. I was seventeen then—and suddenly the concept was there before me, looming over Sheridan Square, already an ironic slap at history when I first spotted the names in 1950.

FOR A POST-WAR PEACEFUL WORLD

ROOSEVELT
*
TRUMAN
*
WAGNER

And underneath their names, in smaller letters, there was that Italian running for the State Assembly. I tried to commit his name, too, to memory. But I failed, even as my eyes closed in on the lettering. I would recite each letter of his name as I stared up at the sign. The small park was filled with the summer-night bodies of other adolescents, of winos, of Villagers out walking their dogs or just passing time until they could maneuver into the Saturday night oblivion and the newsstand rush for the Sunday *Times*. It was the Italian whose name brought up the rear—good soldier in the ranks that he undoubtedly had been—and he was the man I admired. Even if I could not memorize his name, he was the man for me. Whatever he had done to merit inclusion with so august a triumvirate, he was model enough. He embodied a set of possibilities open to every man I knew, and I assumed that he had been painted on the side of that tenement because he was the man we could emulate. The mere presence of his name denied failure. It was a name a man could work to get beyond, for in America, men could transcend all categories whose tyrannies they simply refused to acknowledge. I did not have to know who he actually was or what he had done, how long he'd served or how he met his constituency's needs; it was enough that he had existed, had made his mark. An American. A man among men in a country that belonged to men. He affirmed the prospects before me.

The sign was weathered, the names fading with wind and rain and the indifferent eyes of passersby. A few years later, the sign was whitewashed from the building just off Christopher and Seventh. But the whitewash began to fade as the spot stood unrented and, after a few more years, I could manage to make out the names on the wall. The all-night luncheonette in which I had my first Village assignations disappeared, transmogrified into a bank. The first Village bar I drank in gave way to one of the first expensive Village highrise apartment buildings. But the sign became an anchor, a secret promise between me and America. All through the 1950s, I would drift into the Sheridan Square nights, struggling to make out the letters, to force that name into the borders of my mind one more time—that local who embraced my aspirations. *Listen,* was his message. *And remember. Because this is what it means to be a man in America. Learn. Work. All the proper arrangements. Responsibilities. For you, too. Look at me! This is America, for Christ's sake. A man. Right on the bottom line. A man.* I believed what he told me and burrowed deep within the myths I thought were mine alone until I recognized them, years later, in the eyes of other American men. The indisputable logic of rank, order, privilege. The Italian politico spoke to that logic.

I don't remember when the names disappeared for good. It seems to me that I caught a glimpse of them on the way home from Washington after a demonstration against the Viet Nam war in 1965 By that time, the park covey was filled with stoned runaways and the winos had to fight for elbow room with these newer, younger, more aggressive American refugees. Perhaps there were others who, like me, remembered the names beneath the whitewash. But I doubt it. The Sixties had chosen different models. Manhood was already more of an embarrassment than a promise. All the ersatz offerings— the Kennedys and their professors (whose ranks I had by now joined) and the rock stars and the athletes and the California vegetarians who had come east to bring a new dawn to the rest of America—descended upon the nation with the promise of an endless springtime.

The Italian did not belong here with his clear idea of responsibilities, promise, and expectation. *Listen. And remember.* To this day, I envision him as a small, neat dark-complexioned man, immaculate (perhaps a bit too immaculate) in a gray pin-striped suit with a small white carnation in the lapel. So much time and effort spent washing away the immigrant smell, so much invested in his American-ness, in his responsible manhood. I see him as tough, disciplined, worthy, optimistic, his face molded by the effort to be what he and I and those to the nation born have been taught to admire. A man, after all, is expected to have an idea of style, to move with a controlled sense of his own grace. A man takes on the strain of his struggles and makes of that, too, a personal asset. I want that Italian's intensity, his structured ease of bearing. Like him, I want to be a presence, a substance tempered by memories of how a man comes through.

Today, there is a billboard above the cigar store diagonally across Seventh Avenue. The names are gone for good—no more aspirations of solidarity. The new sign speaks to Now. The heavy-browed rugged face squares off against the glazed faces of the winos and the cars moving down Seventh Avenue. "Come to the country," the newest of American Adams invites. "Man's Country." And then the red-lettered emphasis, the homosexual rush bursting from the need to make one's needs public. *I insist you recognize me!* the face demands. A grudging courage, too. There is something admirable about it, I have to acknowledge that. The sign bleeds red print. The high-cheeked mustachioed face, still sucking on the juices of liberation, invites the world to a homosexual bar. This face speaks of coming out, as if it had been drawn by a child who had memorized how to trace his fantasies in line and space. A man's sex transformed into a role for the moment.

Red letters screaming defiance. That was what we called them, *screamers.* So many names for them then, *screamer, faggot, fruit, bait, queer.* Labels we used attempting to protect our own toughness. Self-conscious manhood bred in schoolyard games. But at least the name-calling let us know what the rules were—the boundaries were marked. It is different now. Everyone searching for the man beneath the skin, as if surface counts for nothing.

Out of the closet, this face has been stripped of shame and silence by an age which embraces the innumerable ways in which one can kiss the heady grace of liberation. It is not merely narcissism that the artist has caught in the poster. His talent is greater than that. This billboard addresses America out of fundamental kinship, and not just here, on Sheridan Square, but throughout the country. For it is America which has created this face and America which has now learned to live with it. Enough tolerance in the country now to touch all. One possesses gender, too, only for the moment. Not a gift, but a momentary possession fought for and won.

Let the father within die! the face cries. It demands the end of all fathers, of the very idea of fatherhood. The cigarette in its hand thrust at the avenue below. Androgynous sexlessness! A new cry splits the air. One does not seek god the father in man's country. Leather-jacketed bodies move beneath the sign with squared-off stiff shoulders and deliberate gait. The homosexual phalanxes nudge one another, pursuing their own time beneath the watchful gaze of the cowboy-hatted queen bee overlooking Sheridan Square. I get out of my car and walk east, away from the face and these new expectations of men in America. I still cannot remember the name of the Italian politico.

II

THE SITUATION IN WHICH MEN find themselves at present in America is comparable to the situation of an athlete whose body, although disciplined and well-conditioned, has decided to call a halt. Desiring rest, it announces its intention to quit. Competition has grown stale and wearisome after all these years, and the athlete must decide whether or not to accept his body's logic. He knows that he has no business pushing against the limits of endurance it has set. Still, there remain the demands of habit and memory. To understand that the body is unwilling to compete any longer is different from accepting that knowledge as final.

Like the athlete, men in America continue to respond to the traditional habits and attitudes expected of a man. And yet, we are told that American men are undergoing a sweeping metamorphosis in which their everyday reality itself is at stake. But even this new reality demands a performance, not a performance that existed in the past but rather one that is part of each man's existence.

You discover that your life still responds to measurements, as if to be born male in America is to be endowed with a tape measure in the mind. You measured how many sewers you could hit in stickball; you measured the size of your cock, the age at which you first got laid, the first binge that you went on; you measured how fast and how far you could run; you measured how much you could earn after school, how independent you could be. And the measurements still exist, even in this *liberated* age. Each statistic is still invested with an authority that must be earned through some kind of performance, however anxiety-ridden and short of the mark it may prove to be.

In retrospect, all that measuring does not seem as unhealthy as we tell ourselves it was. Measurements were emblems of the possible: The world could be absorbed step by step; each standard that you set for yourself could be exceeded. Finally, you learned that you had to control the process of measurement itself. Today, like the athlete, you are at an indeterminate stage, moving toward a consciousness in which limitation is central to your idea of what a man's possibilities are.

It is difficult to see how the measurements of achievement have really changed. The athlete discovers, sooner or later, that his performance now constitutes only the motion of what he was once capable of. Habit is no longer enough. Even if he were still able to command the skill, endurance, and desire he once knew, his performance can never again be the same. He is too conscious of what he has become and of what is demanded of him. He has grown too intimate with himself. It is not merely his body which now wants to acquiesce to the inevitable; it is the very action in which the body is engaged.

The athlete discovers what his body has already learned—that the importance given to performance has begun to dominate his every moment, even as he is aware of its disciplined decline.

Just as performance binds the athlete to a conception of his prowess, it becomes the foremost threat to that prowess. The pattern is repeated for men as they probe their own manhood. Having been conditioned by the need to become what he is, a man discovers that what he is has been called into question. Once his performance as a man has been questioned, its value diminishes. Men of my generation, too young to have fought in World War II and disillusioned by the limitations of all wars fought after that, discover that they have been caught up short by their own myths. Manhood, once a prize to be wrested from a life, is now viewed as an embarrassment, an encumbrance to living successfully. We are no longer sure that our sons can choose their own manhood nor can we yet believe that any other choice they might make can prove as meaningful. We look around ourselves and listen to the ritualized cries of liberation, and we wonder whether the minds of our sons will be levelled with the intensity of this forced joy. Men today seem uncomfortable with their manhood, almost as uncomfortable as they seem when they deny it. As we are caught in the crossfire between change and tradition, liberation itself becomes one more demand to measure up to, one more performance to be witnessed by other men, one more tape measure with which to define the boundaries of manhood.

All the arguments that we should be free from ourselves and from our pasts stand against a background in which performance as a *man* is ridiculed. Terrified of believing what once sustained them, men reduce the very idea of manhood to a quiescent nostalgia, a Saturday afternoon movie meant to control the surge of adolescence. Who can today

remember that middle-class Puritan, our much-berated mem-
ber of the bourgeoisie, who was willing to judge himself, as
well as to permit himself to be judged, by his performance as
man? Who today can read Hemingway without apologizing
for what it was once his glory to believe? The middle-class
man has turned against himself; he condemns himself with
zeal.

"We have met the enemy and he is us!" cries Walt Kelly's
Pogo. We laugh. And then we echo him. We are told that we
are breaking beneath the burdens of responsibilities; we are
told that we are being crushed by the demands of fatherhood;
we are told that we must embrace spontaneity and fulfillment; we are told that we must quest for the newest of
grails—a self that will be relaxed and dazzling, changeable
and calm. And we are told that we have been guilty in all our
roles—father, husband, lover, provider. Quite a judgement for
any Puritan to face. If our position is described as masochis-
tic, we simply point to the general negation of our presence.
And yet, what voice condemns us with a fervor equal to our
own?

Men are condemned for having possessed what used to be
thought of as the *privileges* of manhood. One by one our
accusers step forward: Blacks indict us for the sin of slavery,
for having stolen *their* manhood and tried to incorporate it
into our own; homosexuals say we have denied their model of
being; finally, the fiercest of our accusers steps forward, the
woman we once claimed as our own, outraged by centuries of
subservience and armed with the legitimacy of exploitation,
to demand an auditing of sexual accounts. *"You did this to
me!"* is the cry we hear from all sides. But it is the voice of
woman we have learned to fear most. However shrill her
accusation, we are trapped by our own sense that woman's
sense of outrage is legitimate, her anger justified. In the face
of her onslaught, we defend traditional roles and discover

that we sound like Afrikaaners defending apartheid by boasting of the standard of living enjoyed by *our* blacks.

It is not enough to admit the legitimacy of her charges. We have to look at those charges carefully. The difficulty here is that the very relentlessness of the feminist argument often turns discussion itself to hyperbole. How can any of us deny what is so visibly apparent? How endorse a new stereotype without doing both men and women terrible damage in the process? In a well-known passage from Germaine Greer's *The Female Eunuch,* we are shown woman's savage caricature of what society has made of her.

> In that mysterious dimension where the body meets the soul the stereotype is born and has her being. She is more body than soul, more soul than mind. To her belongs all that is beautiful, even the very word beauty itself. All that exists, exists to beautify her. The sun shines only to burnish her skin and gild her hair; the wind blows only to whip up the color in her cheeks; the sea strives to bathe her; flowers die gladly so that her skin may luxuriate in their essence. She is the crown of creation, the masterpiece. The depths of the sea are ransacked for pearl and coral to deck her; the bowels of the earth are laid open that she might wear gold, sapphires, diamonds and rubies. Baby seals are battered with staves, unborn lambs ripped from their mothers' wombs, millions of moles, muskrats, squirrels, minks, ermines, foxes, beavers, chinchillas, ocelots, lynxes, and other small and lovely creatures die untimely deaths that she might have furs. Egrets, ostriches and peacocks, butterflies and beetles yield her their plumage. Men risk their lives hunting leopards for her coats, and crocodiles for her handbags and shoes.[1]

Few men can stand up under this kind of attack, even when they try to dismiss it as rhetoric. The reality strikes home. If

men have made of women ornaments, have bound her will to
their needs, then they are going to have to understand that
the "prerogatives" they once believed were theirs by inheritance are no longer valid. And it is no longer up to men to
"grant" women what they are demanding. It will take more
than a call for sexual wholeness, with its dreary connotations
of sex counselling clinics and dry obeisance to collective
rights of *fulfillment* (a word which should be cauterized from
the language) before we can stand honestly before each other
again.

The present unenviable situation of men in America does
not derive from the denial of women's complexity. Rather, it
comes from the inability of men to seize those opportunities
given them by the women's movement for a harsh assessment
of who and what they are and of where they stand at this
time.[2] Both self-indictment and self-defense prove inadequate. Never before has there been such a need for men to ask
themselves what *their* situation actually is. An honest debate
over what manhood actually is—not what it should be—is
critical. Can we salvage meaning from the idea of manhood
or must we move instead toward an imprecise sexlessness
whose sole virtue is that it is readily available to all? How
much easier is it to accept myths that demand obedience in
spirit than to encounter the extent to which we have trapped
ourselves by our refusal to meet real terrors in a real world?
How much easier simply to ignore the problem that haunts
the consciousness of all men everywhere—what can we do
with manhood?

The problem seems most pronounced in America, its consequences most crucial. Despite the *Amerika* rhetoric of the
1960s, it is in this country, as Europeans never tire of telling
us, that receptivity to the new is assumed. In Europe, both
men and women have a more difficult time breaking with
tradition. But Americans are so obsessed with the need for

change that the ante is constantly being upped, so that even to think about winning the game proves to be short-lived. This is what drains us, burns us out so quickly. We used to vie with one another to apostrophize manhood and the commerce we created out of it in ways that had little to do with our actual lives. Today we condemn it as the source of all oppression. We seem intent on believing that there are simple solutions to our problems as well as convenient villains upon whom to lay blame.

It is obvious that American men are insecure today: They cannot hide their growing sense of doubt, their nervousness, their consuming belief that somewhere along the line they have failed and have been transformed into the victims of that very sense of manhood they once strove for. Our ideas of what a man is and of what the possibilities of manhood are no longer sustain us, and they no longer generate belief in our capacity to hand our own sense of manhood on to the next generation. The marriages of friends flounder, break apart; acquaintances who had seemed the very pillars of society throw off wife and children and run away to the New Hampshire woods; on the six o'clock news, we watch as an established psychiatrist remakes himself into a woman through a "transsexual operation." None of it surprises us— not the flight to the New Hampshire woods, not the broken marriages, not the rational castration. For we have been told that none of it is to be judged. And yet, how difficult not to notice that all of these escapes are designed to extricate men from the pressing demands of their manhood.

"If I'm grateful for anything," a colleague tells me, "it's that I'm not a young man of twenty today. The poor bastards, I keep thinking that they've never had the stuff for which they're being punished. They've had the sex, but not the pleasure." This is not the time to be young, white, and male in America. Having been judged and found wanting, the

generation retreats. Only the young man able to stand outside
the circle of traditional manhood may have it easier. He at
least can react to the tensions of the time by immersing
himself in the possibility of changing his fate.

But the young middle-class white man in this country cannot even escape through psychological guerrilla warfare. His
dilemma heightens his isolation. Attacked by blacks, homosexuals, women, by virtually all those who insist that their
own problems have been created by him and his ancestors,
his only possible answer to the indictment is silence. If he
insists that he is "different" from his fellows, he discovers
that his receptivity to the indictment becomes a corollary of
his guilt. Acceptance of his sin can never alter the demand for
a new balance in relationships. The victim is never so much
alone as when he admits the error of his ways. He has not
changed the terms of the bargain, nor has he managed to free
himself of the bonds which tie him into his era. Essence, he
discovers, defies metamorphosis. A man is a man, and his
accusers let him know that the nature of the beast cannot be
changed; it can merely be disguised. His accusers invest even
the accidental rancor of the world on his symbolic presence.
He must remain a definable enemy; he cannot be allowed to
disappear.

At the same time that his manhood is called into question,
he discovers that he is not permitted to give it up. Where
manhood once enabled him to sustain a certain idea of himself, something toward which to grow, it is now redefined by
those who insist that they have the right to judge him. Manhood becomes the property of those who damn it as a threat,
and the threat is as open-ended as is the position of being a
man. One is damned if he is and damned if he isn't.

Anyone born male in America between 1920 and 1950
knows that the idea of manhood stained his life. It was an
idea with authority, with mystery. Almost by osmosis, we

learned what a man was *supposed* to be. The notion seemed to hang in the air around us; even unvoiced, it was part of every conversation you had from the age of roughly ten on. The peripheries extended beyond sex to those qualities you could not define—that assertion of will and determination which was supposed to be inherent in manhood. These were the ambiguities which proved so treacherous for most American men. The very lack of definition led to the idea that manhood was as much a state of grace as it was a condition of existence.

Who among us knew what a man was? None of us did, although we all suspected that manhood was something we did not yet possess. And we knew what manhood wasn't. We looked to men of the past and to each other for models of behavior. We tried to match our own qualities or those of our friends and relatives with what we saw on movie screens, heard on the radio, observed on streetcorners and subway cars and Greyhound busses. The rituals were there; they were plausible excuses, forms of conditioning for the future. Even if you could not define manhood, you knew it was out there, waiting to be seized, in a place where language could not really follow. Manhood meant a long coming-of-age, a singular passion which made sense to anyone who sought it. Manhood was something to be taken, a prize to be wrested from an invisible enemy. Hit, hit, and hit again. To survive as a man, you had to establish a solid idea of your selfhood—the collective dream that called for an individual voice. The achievements you claimed as your own were linked to the achievements others claimed as theirs, and so the performance could not be for yourself alone.

How harsh our judgements were. Every man learned to take a certain unabashed pleasure in the strides of his performance and to compare it with others'. Early on you learned to diagnose each other's styles. You were on such intimate terms with fierce unrelenting competition that it became absorbed into the background, the central part of your world. And today, as we try to ferret out those new selves we are so certain we need, we stand ashamed of the old enthusiasms which motivated our quest for manhood.

There is, we find, something terribly awkward about adolescence, something which laughs at the exertions of memory. And yet, we must not cheapen the past, either—we must have some kind of balance. In the long run, we discover that the only thing that can truly be measured is the capacity of the individual man to recognize what he is. Our probing may ultimately leave as much to be desired as did our earlier unrestricted acceptance of the rules of the game—there is, finally, something too facile in the arguments against performance.

Perhaps the competitive urge is not a mere protection against the fearful forces in our lives. Perhaps our ability to be the men we once dreamed of being rests with our untapped capacity to surprise ourselves. We must consider all possibilities, including defeat, to face the demands which today still call for a certain style of execution. There are some games in which there are no winners. A man's behavior is geared to a public response, even at moments of the most intense private fantasy. On the beach at Noordwijk, I discover once again that if you do not insist on the necessity to perform as a man, then there is no choice but to resign yourself to the charity society is willing to mete out when it covers its basic obligations. Most men, fortunately, will not stand for that.

What we sought in performance in our adolescence was a way of grafting self onto situation. We tried to understand the possibilities that were open to us. There was a peculiarly abstract quality to almost everything we did then. Still, there were certain hard guarantees, which made us perform fairly eagerly. The books today which deal with the problems of men seem terribly one-sided in their insistence on the sense of victimization, at least when you recall earlier responses. All right, you did occasionally face the prospect of performance on demand, but was the fear of failure so marked as to make such performance impossible? You hooked your style onto the potential of any situation. Most of the male adolescents I remember anticipated their futures as men with eagerness. Other adolescents, after all, had managed to become men— there was a continuing social context. And what we saw seemed attractive enough to make us want it for ourselves.

Today, we suspect performance. We search for a way to speak about what this manhood to which we aspired really was. We look for answers to the charges levelled against us that point up our admitted confusions, our uncertainty about how successfully we finally measured up. "Speak of me as I am," cries Othello as he is about to kill himself, "nothing extenuate." A model for the besieged consciousness of American men. In a time impatient with our manhood, we discover that we ourselves have been pulled out of all dimension. Sin begins with biology at birth; the stigma we share does not spread from the individual to the group. It is the gender itself that finds that it must defend manhood. Neither class nor race is branded but gender alone, stripped of the fortuitousness of birth, which is made into the devil's mark. As man has sown, so, he discovers, shall he reap. As an old Italian proverb puts it, "The squint-eyed are on all sides accursed."

III

THE GENERATION IN WHICH I GREW UP may have been the last that needed the approval of women. For this reason, among others, we were indeed guilty of making women "objects," however hackneyed the word has by now become. Looking

back, we can see how needing the approval of women created
the retreat from women, a departure which now threatens to
turn into a rout. This need made itself apparent in almost
every aspect of the culture which reflected what we ourselves
were, or at least what we thought ourselves to be. The fiction
we read, the movies we watched, the songs we listened to—all
seemed to affirm the idea that a man's sexuality was a form of
combat with his ultimate self. "Seduction may be baneful,
even tragic," writes Elizabeth Hardwick, "but the seducer at
work is essentially comic."3 However accurate the perception, it was bound to escape the seducer.

We laughed at those comic book and pulp magazine studs,
yet we secretly envied them just as we did the hero of Henry
Miller's books, wondering all the time whether there might
just be something to the fantasy that we ourselves had never
tasted. A man might intend himself as a projection of manhood, his own stud marked off as an enviable rival by all
those fellow men who couldn't get beyond their fantasies;
and in this way he might open himself up to the virtues of his
vice. How pompous sexuality was in the 1940s and 1950s,
and yet how necessary to control the very thing that threatened to control us. We were still careful in the process not to
abdicate the manhood that we sensed could be found at its
center. Our fantasies embodied a culture in which the
woman's willingness to service was taken for granted. And
when we discovered that there were, after all, a significant
number of women who were considerably less than eager to
service our manhood, we took a shocked step backwards. And
then another. And another. And yet another.

It is curious to note that in both of the *Tropic* books, even in
Black Spring, Henry Miller never manages to redeem the self
he claims. And for all the "dirty pages" that we marked off as
adolescents, what we failed to understand was the extent to
which Miller finally sought from sexuality not pleasure but
definition. We envied him his "freedom" as his mythical self

wandered the streets of Paris, cock in hand and fear to the wind, but it was in his sense of definition that he truly served as our representative man. He was each of us, for he had tasted that performance which would be the ultimate test of manhood struggling to get beyond Brooklyn's Fourteenth Ward. The thumbed-down pages of the *Tropic* books were informed by the cheapest of pulp fiction. For sex was a battle fought simultaneously on two fronts—between the sexes and within each sex. The truth of the body invariably demanded a cool temperance of mind which reflected our condition. Both in serious fiction and in the grating pulp pornography, there were always four minds involved in the lovemaking of two bodies— two of them observed while the other two acted.

Curiously enough, it was the risk involved which proved so attractive in sexuality. It is this which makes the retreat from women all the more difficult to explain. For we could be almost monastic in our approach to sexuality, we could stand on the brink of a precipice from which we looked down and saw that life was worthless if a man did not take his chances. In Mailer's "The Time of Her Time," which remains the representative story of the 1950s, the hero, Sergius O'Shaughnessy, feels little pleasure in sex. His manhood is the acceptance of every hole in the mind which fills up with doubt about his capacity, despair about his ability to measure up. The world lies in wait, a trap about to spring on his illusions. And he is as eager to offer his sexual scorecard as any street-corner hero in this nation: "There must have been fifty girls who spent at least one night in the loft," he boasts, exactly like the men I knew scalpcounting early on weekend mornings as if they were bounty hunters and the women their prey. Capacity and courage walked hand in hand; in order to verify their existence, they had to be noted by others. We instinctively understood what Sergius learns—that the value of *scoring* is set by the community of men. And now at a distance provided by shame you watch such motions of the spirit the way you watch the boy you were, extending his tight-knuckled fist to be scraped after losing a game of knucks. Now you know that we would have been better off had we not told each other lies, had we simply acknowledged that only through losing can a man appreciate the fact that to fail is also to live in the risk of love. Poor Sergius, poor manhood.[4]

Still, it does not matter whether we approve of Sergius or of Henry Miller or even of the absurd sexual warriors of pulp fiction. But why was it they who embodied the myths of male sexual performance? My own identification with them was strong enough to prove embarrassing and my imagination was not particularly exotic. The way in which they evoked admiration in me was in their dedication to their own sexual need, for in the 1950s, virtually the only risks available to men were sexual. Miller and Mailer created the imaginative equivalents of our "affliction"—and, along with the pulp fiction hacks, they faced the consequences of their creations more honestly than we did. That manhood and sexuality should be so integrally linked is embarrassing today. But the fact is, they were. A man made the grade or not as lover, sexual capacity was your mark as a man. Our lives testify to that.

But not even in the 1950s did sexual performance exist in a vacuum. If a man pulled the sheets off every encounter he managed to work himself into, he discovered that there was no such thing as good simple sex. For in the 1950s, everything we believed dictated against the simple "being good." Like Sergius O'Shaughnessy and Henry Miller, we believed that sex was the destiny you carved out. Think of what the actual encounter might do to your pride and your willingness to face the new and unexpected. Women insisted on denying our sexual theater games, although they controlled the action as both audience and director.

The war between men and women might have been uncalled-for; still, it was not altogether unhealthy. Sex was that which informed life, and kept men, at least, balanced against the elements of risk in their own lives. In order to understand the gap which divides my generation from the one that followed us, we have to begin with the struggle for sexual supremacy—however embarrassing that struggle may appear today. We can appreciate the justice inherent in the feminist movement and yet still want a world that is not a unisexual marshmallow. In the midst of all the conformity the 1950s bred, there was a recognizable need for something more—the fear of losing a woman you loved would not lead to the substitution of mechanical solutions for the challenge of sex. Failure is always permissible, for failure implies a willingness to accept risk. However crudely a man might choose to live, it was better to live in the risk of love than to stand by paralyzed in an attempt to keep your manhood intact.

IV

AND FATHERHOOD. FOR ME, AT LEAST, birth embodied the deepest ambiguities of manhood. A man wanted the possibilities of consequence for his own sons. At least the possibilities. How distant this is from a generation that sees a parent as a perpetual child reaching for the brass ring on the carrousel, and inevitably missing. Both men and women in America today seem to view children as unnecessary. The problems we acknowledge in sexual relationships are mechanical—problems of technique, movement. How difficult to be weighed down by love or by children. Eros lies buried in the hole in the corner, not in the womb. Few of the glamorous doyens of the feminist movement are mothers; or at least few try to capitalize on that role. Motherhood is a state of servitude to feminists; among contemporary men, it is simply

declassé, like ties and button-down collars. The heroic apoth-
eosis of the new woman transforms the *ewige Weiblichkeit*
into a careerist, the independent woman standing toe to toe
with her independent man, neither of them seeking to com-
plicate their independence with the bindings of family.

The fathers disappear—that is the harshest failure. For me
for the men of my generation, fatherhood was central. How
peculiar that there exists so little fiction of quality in this
country to describe that which we so strongly desired. More
often than not fatherhood is peripheral in literature, a casual
assertion of character, like the color of the pants a man wears.

For of all the rewards of manhood, fatherhood was both the
richest and most fleeting, whether it occurred for the first
time at eighteen or forty-eight. No man, no matter how per-
sistent a lover, could pursue women with quite the same
ardor after he admitted to the responsibility of another life.
The uncommitted man fears involvement not with women
but with the consequences of coming together. That breathing creature is part of a man's own substance, whether created out of obligation or love. Perhaps the women who walk
away from home and children today do so because of our
failure to sustain all the concomitant possibilities of a bring-
ing-into-life. Birth creates out of daily life the kinds of challenges that take precedence over looking into one's own self.
Better than anything else I can name, birth asserts the singularity of the man. His children become his future, and no
matter how much he might shy from the thought, they are an
implicit justification of his manhood. His children are an
investment as they never are for women, since the responsibility for the creation was theirs, and the burden for them
was that much greater.

A fatherhood that is conscious and active creates permanent and irrevocable changes in a man. Fatherhood confirms
reality. It is the one state of being I know of that pierces the
ego's necessary lies. A child's body destroys all the fictions; it

diminishes the self not only in its own sense of importance but also in the space it occupies in the world. At the same time, a father is expected to perform, at least in terms of responsibility for the lives of others, better than he has performed before. Most men would choose sons. At least, they would if they were to speak honestly. Not, I think, because men believe their names must be carried on to guarantee a bath in posterity. And certainly not for any of the traditional roles which sons used to play—warriors, farmers, protectors of a man's old age—all of which have been made obsolescent by that very technology we blame for diminishing the value of our manhood. No, what we seek to perpetuate through our sons is the *condition* of manhood. The immortality we crave is transformed into a collective need, as if fathering sons offered asylum from an age with few other values. The lives of men need structures and children provide them. Looking back, it seems to me as if having children was more important to the men I knew than it was to their wives. Perhaps that was our own version of gender-switching. Obviously, it was the woman whose body carried another body. But the weight of change seemed even greater for the men I knew. We were pulled up short in our lives when our children came, forced to face a different idea of manhood.

"You're not a man until your first child is born," a psychiatrist friend tells me as we sit in a midtown coffee shop. He was forty-three when he had his first child. "No matter what we may say, that's the true separation of the self from its parents. The rest is window-dressing. Styles of fucking, the question of how successful you are professionally, even the extent of the courage you possess—none of it counts as much as when you admit responsibility for another life." He leans back, a sharp-faced man with distant eyes.

"Then why," I ask, "do so many men run away from exactly that responsibility today? My students sure as hell don't want to be fathers. Every newspaper I pick up tells me that

impotence is like a damn plague. You've told me that yourself." He nods. "So how is being a father an endorsement of
manhood? If men really are frightened of women today, then
being responsible for children would absolutely terrify them.
There's nothing left even to back into. All their myths have
been destroyed."

"But not the need for children. Even macho derives its
strength from the myth of the father."

"But when fatherhood is simple tyranny?"

"You may want to eliminate something because that's what
you can't be, but that doesn't necessarily mean the idea, the
attraction of the thing, is dead, right?" He lights a cigarette,
falls silent. "Speak to some of the young men who come to
my office. It's not that they don't *want* to be fathers. It's just
that the thing itself seems so complex, so overwhelming.
They want it as much as we did.

"For us, to be fathers meant that we had arrived at the
independence that manhood was supposed to give us. But the
'father' is dead today. Fatherhood is dead as an idea."

I shake my head. "I'd like to speak to some of your patients.
I know very few men between the ages of eighteen and thirty-
five who are particularly eager to have kids. I don't see anything going on with them except the need to give that *me* a
little more sugar."

"And the next generation?" my friend asks. "Your sons?"

I shrug. "I don't know," I confess. "Sometimes, when I
watch adolescent boys, I get the idea that they are going to
swing the pendulum so far back that what we thought of as
tough will be their version of a pussycat. They're looking for
models, only the models have disappeared. For you and me,
fatherhood was essential. But to them?"

"Just to survive," he interrupts. "Is that what they're
after? Jesus, it would be nice if they managed to land somewhere in between."

V

I REMEMBER SITTING, SWEATING in my own silence and wondering how I arrived in this hospital lobby. I try to harness the energy of events, but feel drained of all sensation. I am not even afraid for my wife and my yet-unborn child. It is simple, I tell myself, multitudes of women give birth each day. Even the births that are premature, as this one is to be, are now fairly routine.

It is two-thirty in the morning. I am sitting in the polished tiled lobby of the maternity pavilion. I smoke one cigarette after another and listen to the activity around me. Two other fathers-to-be sit in the lounge with me. One is expecting twins. The other is reading *The Green Sheet.* His pencil stabs the paper with dark slashes, quick notations. He circles the names of jockeys, and I am impressed by the faultlessness of his motions. I do not understand why he is so unaware of where we are. Unknown bodies are about to be delivered into the world. He looks up from the paper. He is about ten years older than I am, and he momentarily calms my growing anxiety with a glance. "It's nothing," he says. "Absolutely nothing."

I am grateful for the conversation. "I'm nervous," I confess. "I don't know what to expect."

He snorts. "Only natural. Listen, it's harder to hit a winner in the sixth at Hialeah. Christ, I'd rather eat a snake than bet without good information. Don't worry. I been here before. Six times. It's like stairs. You go up, you go down."

"What's it feel like?" I ask.

"*I* never had one," he laughs. He studies my face, as if surprised that his attention can be diverted from charting winners at Hialeah. "You mean, being a father?" I nod. "You know, it's not something you really think about very much. Only you suddenly got to do what was done for you. It's there; you've made it. So now there's another one you've got to feed. That's the way it is. You got to take care of it. So then you're a man—no tricks to the thing. Even if the kid should come out lousy. Of course, I'm talking about a kid who has everything where it should be. Up here, too." He taps his head with his forefinger, noticing for the first time the crutches which I have stacked against the wall. "And healthy. You want it should be healthy. Because it's yours and you're responsible for it. What else is a man for?"

He turns back to *The Green Sheet,* no longer looking at me, as if he has offered more than he had wanted to. "I'm not nervous no more. Only I'm still wondering. It's a little crazy, you know. My oldest son, he's fourteen years old. And I'm still wondering what kind of father I'll be." He snorts. "Maybe that's why I like the horses."

You want it should be healthy. I want a son. Behind the closed doors in my mind, I want a son. In a world of victims and users, what is the glory of man? A singular creature. Men do not feel. Not true. They feel too much. Only they feel in the silence, isolated from the world, from each other, where all they can touch is the rhythm of their own breathing, that reassurance of their fears and hopes racing through the mind—flashes of expectation on which to pin a man's coming-of-age.

Do I want the same for my yet-unborn son? Yes, I do. I want to will him his kingdom, the lost kingdom, in which he will race against the pressures of his own fantasies, his own needs. I pledge you joy in becoming a man. And sorrow and pain and silence, too. I offer you the need to wrestle with ghosts and demons, those you will create and those already waiting for you, that will seize you on your way. Your grandfather, my father, thinks of himself, of all men, as *shtetl* peasants captured out of their time, chained to their capacity for work and the need to make a living. But there is so much more. There is the grammar of the body. Good, better, best. Yours. A man survives. With and without illusions, facing his fears and fleeing them.

I light another cigarette. My gut is churning cold now, I feel sick. "Takes long," I say aloud. The father of six grunts, ignores me. The other man snatches the opening. His fat face already running down, chin sliding into chin. I wonder whether he is going to pull rank on me, too.

"Each is different," he assures me in a textbook voice. But he is eager to share with me. He sees us as allies. Nor is he so far removed from my state. He has one child already, a girl of three, whose picture he happily shows me. But now he is waiting for twins, or so he and his wife have been told. The voice mingles pride and caution. "The first time it's a sweat. This time I'm calm. What worries me is the afterwards. Three kids. It's a responsibility."

We drift into silence. I fall asleep, dreaming of my son-to-be, spinning my confusions out. In the dream, I am my own father. I speak with the accent of the *shtetl*, I hold the world at bay, I surrender to the driven workhorse within. Work and sweat. I find myself lifting barrels of smoked salmon across a baseball field. As I carry them, the fish turn to sand, the barrels grow heavier. My son, whom I cannot see but who I know looks exactly as I do now, is standing behind me. I can feel him there, but I cannot see him. I simply know he is shaking his head, as if to say, "This is not a proper performance. There has to be something better." I struggle with the barrels, enraged, determined to show him how strong I am. And then I hear the howling and my son, myself, disappears, and then I hear, "I want to see a doctor! Let me see a fucking doctor!"

I am pulled from the dream and awake abruptly. The man
with the racing form is gone, and the other man who is
expecting twins is staring wide-eyed and terrified at two hospital guards and a short Hispanic man whom they are trying
to hold. He howls, "I want a fucking doctor! Let me get my
hands on one of those bastards!"

"Show us your clinic card!" one guard demands.

"How can we help you," the other guard asks, as he tries to
grasp the man's shoulder, "if you don't show us your card?"

"I'll show you!" the man screams. He drops a brown paper
bag that says FINAST in red letters. I am wide awake by now.
"There's my card, you bastards!" It looks like a cat that has
been run over by a car. Nausea riding my gut, I find myself
wondering whether it is male or female. And then, unable to
throw up, I grab my crutches and push off the chair while the
man breaks free and runs off howling down the corridor. I
carefully avoid the fetus on the floor. The expectant father of
twins is crying, fat face cradled in his hands. Then I see my
friend Jerry, my wife's obstetrician, walking towards me,
right hand outstretched. "It's a boy," he announces. "Talk
about intuition. I knew it in my hands when I first felt it in
the womb."

VI

IT IS NOT THE TRAUMA OF BIRTH that molds either a son's
legacy or a father's performance. Still, I find myself back in
that hospital lobby, and I wonder whether the insane rage of
that man with the fetus in the brown paper bag was not the
eye of the cyclone. That man must have been caught, committed, analyzed, reanalyzed, soothed by the doctors, turned
inside and out, until dreams of sons evaporated entirely.
Other sons were born to other fathers on that drizzly Decem-

ber evening in 1962; other future men were brought into a world in which they were no longer certain of what it was they would be called upon to do. The feverish eye in which the father's need is reflected is not a quiet pool of disguised contentment but rather all the thwarted ambition, the toughened desire, the sullen gift of the human with which he lives. Having brought a son into a world in which manhood is viewed as a disease, the father discovers that he must now explain its origins, those rude awakenings and hard surprises, that surplus of expectation. And for whose destiny?

Perhaps I might have chosen a more auspicious time for my son's entry into this American world, but I did not know it on that December evening. Perhaps he, too, still might push beyond narcissism and face the true complexities of what he could become, even in a world where such needs could easily be dismissed. It was not, after all, that his beginning was inauspicious but that the time of his birth was off. Under the best of circumstances and in the best of times, it was difficult enough to be the man you set out to capture. But now for my fifteen-year-old son, there was the added threat of living in a country where gender was an implied judgement of the man. I imagine my son at the moment of his birth pointing his finger in accusation at me. "Listen," I can hear him say. "You are going to protect me, teach me—which is I suppose something you have to do for your own. I'm willing to face the tests, too. I'm willing to believe that performance doesn't make a man less than human and that I have to work at my own endurance. Only you'll never be able to explain how I become that kind of man when he's been dismissed as old-fashioned, ready for the dustbin of history, dear father. You say that women are right, they should be able to claim what they want, too. So where does that leave me? Heading down the plastic chute into an egalitarian sexlessness? Why not draw me a map that's useful? No double-entry sexual book-keeping. I want to know what you learned, you and your generation, and what you did with it. I want to know why I should want what you needed if it is so different now. My God, men are finally getting all the attention, and they're more afraid now than when they thought they were being ignored. I don't want to make others my victims any more than you did—not woman, not man. But I still want to live *against* what's out there. I want to own my life. Isn't that what you've been telling me being a man is?''

My son's monologue makes me uneasy. With so much talk of liberation in the air, why do men cautiously feel for their freedom like Samson feeling for the pillars of the temple? Never has more been written in praise of the independent man. Why, then, are we still so nervous about the results? We flee women, we run from ourselves, we avoid each other. We envy the very women we run from, we scourge ourselves with their accusations, for the manhood performance traps us again and again with its impermanence.

FOOTNOTES

1. Germaine Greer, *The Female Eunuch* (New York, 1971), pp. 51–52.

2. There have, of course, been books which purport to do exactly this, most notably Warren Farrell's *The Liberated Man*. But Farrell's book is the very antithesis of the kind of assessment I am calling for here. It embodies that tedious *mea culpa* sexual rhetoric that is our own time's version of sociological zilch. Farrell has simply switched the roles and made women the good guys and men the bad guys. That his book could even be taken seriously seems to me a sad commentary on the state of reality between the sexes.

3. Elizabeth Hardwick *Seduction and Betrayal* (New York, 1975), p. 187.

4. Sergius lives, as Kate Millett pointed out in *Sexual Politics,* a life of intense self-inflation—and this makes him more than a bit embarrassing as our generation's representative man. Sex is a form of combat about which he is so earnest that its humor leaves him infuriated. Still, even after one admits to the truth of Ms. Millett's charge that "like any soldier hardened by his own side's agitprop, he can also fall into the jingoism of the sexual patriot," Sergius remains representative in that his need to "inflict" his sexual presence is at war with whatever deeper humanity he possesses. And it is exactly here, it seems to me, that he moves beyond that two-dimensional sexual posturing which is all Ms. Millett is willing to grant him. One may wish that Mailer had been able to temper Sergius's need to reach beyond himself through sex with the recognition that women had similar needs. It is a pity that he has to drown women in that age-old manhood fantasy of endowing them with the gift of orgasm. Still, to try to score critical points at either Mailer's expense or at the expense of his creation is to miss what is central to his story. In every word Sergius utters, the reader is made

conscious of what women do to men in America through the sheer fact of their existence. It would be impossible to write a story such as "The Time of Her Time" today, which is one of the reasons why the generation in which I grew up may have been the last to need the approval of women.

Chapter Three
The Landscape of American Manhood

It was about this time I conceived the bold and arduous project of arriving at moral perfection. I wished to live without committing any fault at any time; I would conquer all that either natural inclination, custom, or company might lead me into. As I knew, or thought I knew, what was right and wrong, I did not see why I might not always do the one and avoid the other. But I soon found I had undertaken a task of more difficulty than I had imagined. While my care was employed in guarding against one fault, I was often surprised by another; habit took the advantage of inattention; inclination was sometimes too strong for reason.

—*Benjamin Franklin*, The Autobiography

So, we are told, the New Hollander goes naked with impunity, while the European shivers in his clothes. Is it impossible to combine the hardiness of these savages with the intellectualness of the civilized man?

—*Henry David Thoreau*, Walden

A REAL MAN

Scarsdale: *Three cheers and a tip of my hat to the Texan who shot and killed one of the two muggers who attacked him at the Hilton. He should have been given a gold-plated key to the city on a silver platter! Thank you, sir, and the next time please shoot both creeps. And to all those cowed, disarmed sheep who live in New York. Kindly note that at least in the rest of the country there are men left.*

—*"Crime Victim," "The Voice of the People,"*
New York Daily News, *January 26, 1978*

I

MANHOOD IN AMERICA HAS ARRIVED at a peculiar destiny: As a condition it may yet prove to be as suspect as an inherited disease.

American men have traditionally been expected to be as pragmatic as Franklin, as tough as Thoreau, and as independent and resourceful as that "real man" from Texas, but today they learn to parody the very idea of a meaningful manhood.

Ideas about manhood are legacies from both personal and collective histories that bridge past and present. Neither men nor their encounters with the world simply spring into being and stand isolated against their time. Man's passions and his limitations all testify to the endurance of the past, even at a time when men deny the power of that past. This has been a particularly difficult lesson for the American man to learn since he has traditionally kept history at arm's length. Only a nation of men convinced that their "newness" testified both to the inadequacy of prior ages and to men's ability to liberate themselves from that past's dead hand could conceivably believe that history might be irrelevant. European man might seek an end to the nightmare of history, but he knows that he cannot dismiss it; at best, he can work to change its impact.

But for the American, the geography of the moment provided the landscape against which a man's destiny might be determined. The sheer size of the country, the immense distances which separated individuals from each other, dictated our conceptions of manhood. The availability of space created a sense of boundlessness that seized all men and frightened many. It was always a problem to strike a balance between the demands of the environment and the obligations a man owed to himself. In Europe, the reconciliation of savage and civilized man that Thoreau desired was a sentimental idea; in America, it was an available experience.

American men witness their arrival in the world as an image of the self hurled against an environment that is open and hostile, receptive and distant. In the most densely packed American cities, boys grew to manhood knowing the extent to which they, too, were part of the western myth—what R. W. B. Lewis described as "the image of a radically new personality, the hero of the new adventure: an individual emancipated from history, happily bereft of ancestry, untouched and undefiled by the usual inheritances of family and race; an individual standing alone, self-reliant and self-propelling, ready to confront whatever awaited him with the aid of his own unique and inherent resources."[1] They did not have to read the Leatherstocking Tales or understand Frederick Jackson Turner's frontier thesis to know this.[2]

Both the eighteenth and nineteenth centuries found in American life possibilities of human existence which had never before been stated so clearly. Given the immensity of space and the availability of land, ordinary men could conceive of achieving mastery over their dominions. European insularity breaks down when confronted by American boundlessness. "*Amerika,*" cries Goethe, "*du hast es besser.*" And no one is more eager to believe him than the American man. History wants to impose boundaries on him, but his claim is that by ignoring the boundaries he breaks the tyranny of history. The "fresh green breast of the new world" that Fitzgerald evokes so elegiacally at the end of *The Great*

Gatsby was a promise that men really believed they could experience in America. And the very idea of such a promise connoted the corollary idea of the "newness" of the American man—self-sufficient, ready to adapt to circumstance, capable of dealing with the wilderness before him because it demanded what he possessed—endurance, determination, and a willingness to get beyond his origins, to live without the encumbrance of the past and its traditions.

De Crèvecoeur addresses himself to that sense of opportunity in a passage that pushes beyond the page, its desire for the "new" tempered only by the uncertainty inherent in the unknown.

> From nothing to start into being; from a servant to the rank of master; from being the slave of some despotic prince, to become a free man, invested with lands, to which every municipal blessing is annexed! What a change indeed! It is in consequence of that change that he becomes an American. The great metamorphosis has a double effect, it extinguishes all his European prejudices, he forgets that mechanism of subordination, that servility of disposition which poverty had taught him; and sometimes he is apt to forget too much, often passing from one extreme to the other.[3]

He is the "new man" who feels he can obliterate history. And yet, the prospect has its dangers. De Crèvecoeur cautions that he is "apt to forget too much." And the consequences of such forgetting pull him back to his European origins and check his newly discovered aspirations of a more independent existence. But a point of view, like a habit, can become a collective property. Our evolving nation was composed of men who grew to believe that it was necessary to rid themselves of many of the restrictions of their European forefathers. The American wilderness demanded physical capacity and intellectual adaptation; it promised men that they might master the environment and be truly independent. A man's talents had little to do, as de Crèvecoeur noted, with birth or background. He might endow his resourcefulness on something larger than his station in life.

The depth of this sense of each man's potential is, I believe, what continues to account for the fascination which Fitzgerald's *The Great Gatsby* still holds for us: "For a transitory enchanted moment man must have held his breath in the presence of this continent, compelled into an aesthetic contemplation he neither understood nor desired, face to face for the last time in history with something commensurate to his capacity for wonder." It is the capacity which rescues Gatsby himself from a parochial mediocrity, which transforms the story of a slightly ludicrous gangster into a protagonist who speaks for each man in America at a cautious time in history. *Gatsby,* which is actually a two-dimensional novel, has been analyzed with all the critical ammunition once reserved for religious exegesis, undoubtedly because it speaks to the possibility of self-creation, man placing his selfhood at the forefront of existence. "You can't repeat the past," Nick warns Gatsby, after he has discovered why Gatsby lives like some shrouded Caesar in the marketplace, dreaming his ambitions away in his "factual imitation of some Hotel de Ville in Normandy." And Gatsby's incredulity echoes each American man's urges: "Can't repeat the past? Why of course you can."

This belief is a standard affliction among American men. For only an American believes that he can set history right and project himself to the top of his surroundings. Gatsby's dreams are vulgar and romantic and meretricious, but they are also rooted to his idea that manhood is the sum of one's ambition and daring. He has been taught that he is capable of forging the man within and trying it out as one tries out a model airplane. And what American boy, rich or poor, has not stated his ambitions and made his dreams concrete through the intricacies of schedules and charts? The self's defiance of history is incorporated even into time-and-motion studies in America.

```
Rise from bed  ........................... 6.00 A.M.
Dumbbell exercise and wall-scaling  .... 6.15–6.30 A.M.
Study electricity, etc.  ................ 7.15–8.15 A.M.
Work  ........................... 8.30–4.30 P.M.
Baseball and sports  ................. 4.30–5.00 P.M.
Practice elocution, poise
   and how to attain it  ................ 5.00–6.00 P.M.
Study needed inventions  ............. 7.00–9.00 P.M.
```

GENERAL RESOLVES

No wasting time at Shafters or (a name, indecipherable)
No more smokeing or chewing.
Bath every other day
Read one improving book or magazine per week
Save $5.00 [crossed out] $3.00 per week
Be better to parents

Of course, it is easy to laugh at this kind of thing. But are the ambitions of the young Jay Gatz any less American than the laundry lists of ambition that mark the lives of American men since colonial times? "I made a little book," wrote Franklin, that most profoundly American of the Founding Fathers, "in which I allotted a page for each of the virtues." And he does, creating a chart on which he can record "the habit of that virtue so much strengthened."[4] The progress report of an American man. The world, after all, is meant to be measured, for how else can the man of action and the man of morality join together in a common superiority? In America, a man must reign over circumstance. For it has been left to him—and, he believes, to him alone—to cancel history through the force of his ambition, the thrust of his physical prowess, and the acceptance of his immense potential.

II

AMERICAN MANHOOD REMAINED a defined and simple role even after the frontier was settled. As long as any part of the landscape stood waiting to be conquered, a man might take both it and his role in subduing it for granted. Not until well into the twentieth century were American men forced to wonder what being a man means. Writers of the eighteenth and nineteenth centuries, living in their pre-Freudian naïveté, might wonder about courage, capacity, even the ability to sustain the integrity of the self in the face of their dreams. But these are problems for the individual self; they do not address themselves to the issue of roles. For manhood can still be assumed; a sexual role is still one of the givens of existence. Men struggled with conscience, with government, with the power of other men, with the wilderness—but they did not struggle with the question of exactly what being a man in America meant. Roles were sufficiently defined so that a man might match his ambition against them. Alternatives to manhood could only be expressed furtively, as they are in Melville's "Bartleby the Scrivener." The protagonist refuses to serve the traditional masculine imperatives of pre–Civil War America and his failure as a man is viewed as a form of resistance to tyranny. But such a story is not characteristic of American attitudes. Before our own times and the reign of the anti-hero, what American man could have accepted a view of "dropping out" which would make him different from and better than other men? The primary expression of manhood in the last century was physical, since man in this country was of necessity a physical being. H used the world, would not be used by it.

Our history can be read, in part, as the record of the ways in which man imposed his physical presence on the landscape. One of the reasons why the American man was able to worship "success" so openly was that he understood it as deriving from his physical power. The strength of his body was his passport.

Today this embarrasses us, and we attempt to "spiritualize" the body. But the reality is that American experience knotted the individual man to an idea of the landscape as enemy; consequently, he is defined by others and he defines himself by his ability to manipulate the *real* physical world. How easy it is to forget that there was a real American wilderness that forced men to seek the levels of their own manhood. If men pillaged the environment, they also confronted themselves *in* it. And they expected their sense of worth, their manhood, to emerge from that confrontation.

The combination of civilized man and savage that Thoreau wanted was already apparent before the Civil War: The frontiersman who was to be emulated by generations of American boys was already an essential presence. He was a powerful role model—strong enough even to become an object of caricature. As Henry Nash Smith writes about the introduction of the figure of Buffalo Bill to the American reading public in the *New York Weekly* in 1869, "the *persona* created by the writers of popular fiction was so accurate an expression of the demands of the popular imagination that it proved powerful enough to shape an actual man in its own image."[5] Even today, the frontiersman's image must be taken into account. No other figure seized the collective imagination so powerfully, and no other figure held on so tenaciously as a role model for men in America. In the frontiersman's life, or at least in the way in which that life was mythicized for the reading public, landscape and character achieve a synthesis where one is activated by the other. The frontiersman still provides the essential masculine image for those who see American manhood as a history of imposing power upon others. It is his image which so often provides the rhetorical framework for conservative politicians worried about this nation's declining strength. And it is his image which also provides the embryonic outline for feminist attacks on the American man's idea of what his manhood should be.

Curiously enough, his is an essentially sexless manhood. He seems today a peculiar "child of Nature" (as Byron speaks of Daniel Boone in *Don Juan)* in the severe restrictions he imposes upon his sexuality. No fig-leafed statue could be more coy. The frontiersman's manhood consists of his ability to take from the natural landscape. He is willing to battle the mercurial moods with which Nature demonstrates power; he is not particularly willing to battle his internal emotional life with women. All physical skills are available to him, except those needed by the lover. In his most memorable fictional creation, as Cooper's Leatherstocking, he is relentlessly asexual, so that Natty Bumppo's death in *The Prairie* becomes not the death of a single man but a means of incorporating legend into national fact. But Natty is deified only because he poses no physical threat to the culture that adulates him—at least none that it cannot handle. His skills are those of the trapper, the hunter, the woodsman. He has kept women at a distance; indeed, he has kept other white men at a distance. His manhood has been constructed upon his courage, his physical prowess, and his religion of nature, all absorbed into a primitive Christianity. However, he has been forced to accept the existence of others; he has not really been loved by women, except by Judith Hutter, who is morally beyond the pale. Balzac called him a "moral hermaphrodite," a phrase that effectively captures his diffused sexlessness. Natty Bumppo instructed future generations of American men on how to compartmentalize themselves by placing their sexuality at a distance from their inner lives.[6]

Of course, it is not only the frontiersman who has fragmented his life into the physical and the spiritual, although his image reinforces the concept. One is tempted to claim that our contemporary obsession with sexuality is as much a legacy of the past as was man's supposed denial of his passions. Well into the twentieth century, the images of the sexes provided to the public avoid any intimation of adult sexuality. However infantile, the Hollywood cowboy of the 1930s addressed the antiseptic sexlessness that had been made ours by inheritance. Between savage and civilized man, between the landscape as battlefield and the landscape as pastorale, the American man discovers that he is trapped in an essentially asexual physicality.

But his character remains. And his independence. In the blending of geography with the idea of self-sufficiency, the frontiersman gives a hard center to American beliefs about manhood. And what is striking about the frontiersman's heroic image is the extent to which his virtues could be emulated. The Daniel Boone whom we meet in John Filson's eighteenth century *Kentucke* may be idealized, but he is never removed from either the range of experience or of anticipation available to other men. All Americans of that era were expected to exploit the opportunities available to them. When asked whether the dying Andrew Jackson would go to heaven, one of his slaves is said to have answered, "He will if he wants to." In an environment so completely open to exploitation, the individual had only himself to define as success or failure. The quixotic whims of nature, the enemies surrounding him, the struggle between classes—the American man managed to accept all of these as real and yet remained convinced that each individual had the capacity, if not the obligation, to control his own future.

Men eyed their own capacities when they searched for

heroes. The Daniel Boone of myth and fiction struggled with the Daniel Boone of historical reality, a man not unlike those surrounding him. Each man in America envisioned himself as the other. For in American life, each man was expected to keep alternatives in mind even when he struck out in one particular direction. The notion of beginning again, of starting over, is linked to a restless irritation with the necessity of making choices, and thereby limiting oneself. The essence of manhood could be found in the choices a man made, but he was always aware of the paths he had not taken. The obligations of his manhood might lie in the direction he had not chosen, in the things he had not done, in the roads he could not bring himself to walk. Man in America is possessed by an idea that he stands opposed to the world—and this, too, is part of the frontier legacy. The American man was seen by de Tocqueville and other European travellers to nineteenth-century America as independent and conformist, heroic and mendacious, energetic and restrictive.

Both de Tocqueville and Harriet Martineau, two of the more astute European observers, discovered here a manhood so self-consciously assertive and confident that it seemed suspicious.[7] The nineteenth-century American viewed himself as the most singular creature on the face of the earth. His European analysts saw him as far more limited, a man whose sense of his destiny was as inflated as his sense of his own importance. He called upon the institutions he had created to organize those virtues he had garnered from the frontier, and the greater the distance between himself and the frontier, the louder the call. He has an unequivocal faith in his own singularity. Tied to the landscape he seeks to dominate by his opportunism, he is unable to see himself realistically. He is rude, he is a braggart, he refuses the idea of limitation. Only his belief in his uniqueness and his willingness to test that uniqueness saves him. His manners might be comic, but his sense of his own worth as a man proves refreshing. Behind his bragging, he may be, indeed, a better, more independent, man than his European counterpart. This suspicion adds to European irritation with him.

Compared to European man, he seems shallow, too simple a creature to be taken seriously. But his is an assertive simplicity, with an enviable kind of assured liveliness. He assumes the supremacy of his own physical prowess. He invents public relations even before the need is apparent. He decides that a man is whatever he declares himself to be. In a country in which success has less to do with a man's past than with his capacity, even bragging can be put to use. He could be, as Davy Crockett was, self-taught and idealistically motivated, yet he could still deftly sustain illusions about his life with the crassest verbal manipulations. Once he had managed to demonstrate his manhood for others, no boast was too extreme. And if English ladies didn't like what they found, well, then, they could take the next boat back to England. Even his humor was his own.

> I'm that same David Crockett, fresh from the backwoods, half-horse, half-alligator, a little touched with the snapping turtle; can wade the Mississippi, leap the Ohio, ride upon a streak of lightning, and slip without a scratch down a honey locust; can whip my weight in wildcats,— and if any gentleman pleases, for a ten dollar bill, he may throw in a panther,—hug a bear too close for comfort, and eat any man opposed to Jackson.[8]

Such humor catches a man mocking his own myth, and it also points up his need for independence. To a certain extent, it is a humor which defines the quality of his manhood by the distance it places between his achievements and his ambitions. And it is attractive, for self-mockery restores him to a human scale, capable of laughing at his own absurdities. American heroes are rarely allowed to be pompous (although this humorous perspective has somewhat diminished in our own time), and they are never allowed to get so far ahead of the ordinary man as to seem outside his real experience.

Compared to his European contemporary, nineteenth-century American man seems both freer and more restricted. All through the century, as David Riesman notes, "travelers' reports from Europe impress us with their unanimity. The American man is said to be shallower, freer with his money, friendlier, more uncertain of himself and his values, more demanding of approval than the European."[9]

In the great autobiographies of European culture, we are always made aware of the splits between one idea of a man's function and another: in St. Augustine, between flesh and spirit; in Cellini, between artist and lover; in Rousseau, between free man and neurotic. But the greatest of American autobiographies, and the one that is probably most representative—Benjamin Franklin's—offers a life that is both purposeful and planned. The author saw men as the sum total of their talents, but he accepted the idea that all talents were available to all men, subject only to individual determination. Morality emanated from within each man. Puritan theology had dissipated for Franklin to encompass morality without either a metaphysics or a teleology. His imagination was geared to the pragmatic, to the possibility of abundance. And while he was a far more daring and inventive man than we generally acknowledge, he approached even opportunity with a certain proprietary caution. His belief in hard work and planning prevented him from seeing the extent to which life could be tragic. In his *Autobiography*, he holds his emotions in check by refusing to examine their realities. His manhood is limited, as Melville noted, because of his insistence on order; he is a man who is "everything but a poet." His vision is bounded on all sides by the self he creates—like the frontiersman, he reasons from the landscape outwards. All men can conquer if they begin with themselves; all environments can be managed. And so can the lives of men.

III

MANHOOD IN GENERAL, and American manhood in particular, has of late been accused of aggression—both upon the outside world and upon the inner self. Men are no greater than the spaces they inhabit, and so the American man attacks his environment. He may sentimentalize the landscape, but that does not change his need to make it over. How differently the frontiersman and the Indian looked upon nature. For the Indian, nature embodied permanent force, to be placated in its wrath and loved for its generosity. The idea of nature as something that had to be *conquered* was inconceivable. But the frontiersman approached the wilderness with the knowledge that others were to follow. No matter how much he himself may have revolted against civilized existence, his very presence on the frontier was an indication that it was doomed, and that he would be responsible for its extinction. Nature would have to change so that man might change. In the traps set by the Mountain Men, one discovers rudimentary railroads and cities.

By the Civil War, the aggression upon nature has become an aggression upon the self. Only recently have scholars begun to turn their attention from its political, economic, and military consequences to the War's impact upon the ideals and aspirations behind American life.[10] The post–Civil War American man suddenly finds himself confronted by new forces which are designed to test the new man. At the point of his greatest success, he discovers that he must search for new areas of conquest. He must discover how to unleash his aggressiveness on an America that has already been changed and that he will soon change further, almost beyond recognition. Power, assurance, and discipline are harnessed in the service of an energy that feeds on itself. Men of power and substance after the Civil War did not really lead personal lives. In the process of achieving power, they created a potential for wealth greater than that of any other culture in history. New forces, new technological processes could be used in a further attempt to exploit the landscape and impose a different order upon the dwindling wilderness. Men in America possessed a power that lay beyond their understanding, and yet power, as Henry Adams noted, "when wielded by abnormal energy is the most serious of facts."[11]

This newly discovered power defines the American man after the Civil War. At times, he is its victim, twisted by the will of fashion, forced to accommodate his existence to its demands. But he grows accustomed to the mystery of what he possesses. In the vast vulgarity of the Gilded Age, patterns of wealth emulate fantasy. By the standards of European wealth, of course, the inventors and merchandisers who came to power after Lincoln's death were ludicrous. "Except in the area of business, they invented nothing at all—not a book, not a philosophy, not a religion, not a scientific discovery, not a single new mode of art or culture, but only an occasional machine, like the reaper and harvester."[12] Theirs is a manipulative energy, a specifically masculine energy, one that, when it appears in women, is looked at both as sexual and strange, a violation of the way in which nature had intended the world. Regardless of what they offered to the world, these men were set up as examples. At no other time, before or since, were the rich in as enviable a position in American life. Even the ludicrous quality of their play could demonstrate what men might achieve with energy. It is tempting to view their lives as a kind of collective sport brought about by the growth of predatory capitalism. They seemed to embody the new mechanical forces they controlled, or this, at least, accounts for their hold upon the popular imagination. The manufacturers and bankers who came to dominate American life between the Civil War and the First World War substituted energy for thought, for manners, even for the idea of what they came to call "society."

Energy in America went beyond even wealth. In a well-known chapter on Ulysses Grant in *The Education of Henry Adams*, it is the profound effect of Grant's energy that makes Adams feel like a rather petulant child who has suddenly discovered that there are bigger boys on the block who are capable of beating him up. "When in action he was superb and safe to follow; only when torpid was he dangerous."[13] Adams considers Grant an anachronism; he portrays him as if he were a pure biological specimen of aggressive manhood. But Grant was simply a magnification of both the assets and liabilities of other men in the country he led. Even to more impartial observers than Adams, Grant is transformed into the essential American man, in whom both personal style and the quality of achievement have been Americanized. Adams viewed him as distant, lacking imagination, at times even brutal in his directness. And yet, seen from the perspective of our own time, he emerges more and more as the man whose independent selfhood, derived from the frontier, embodies the relationship of man to environment that characterized the American. Edmund Wilson called his *Memoirs* "a unique expression of the national character,"[14] and it is interesting to examine Grant's *Memoirs* alongside both Adams's *Education* and Franklin's *Autobiography*. For the unity we see between the man of thought and the man of action in Franklin, has by now been split in half—so that we have Grant's forceful energy, which lacks understanding, and Adams's pensiveness, which reduces the idea of action to a question of pedigree.

Grant has accepted the idea of what his countrymen thought a man should be—an overwhelming force. Today when the idea of this kind of energy is under renewed attack, there is something curiously refreshing about his character. He possesses *manliness* as the nineteenth century understood

the word, an idea perhaps as valid as the idea of public
service which motivated the Adams family. For the post–
Civil War American man, it was simply natural to assume
that power and self-assurance commanded energy, whereas
Adams had viewed energy as the property of mechanics. His
Education, while it is among the great American life stories,
possesses the kind of whining irritation and sense of displace-
ment that makes his suspicion of energy questionable. Franklin combines intelligence with action; Grant creates of action
a form of intelligence; but Adams simply withdraws from a
world whose greatest shortcoming is its refusal to recognize
that he is as special as he believes he is. His concept of
manhood has too much to do with what was expected of an
Adams, a rather European legacy of family ties and
responsibilities.

> His world was dead. Not a Polish Jew from Warsaw or
> Cracow—not a furtive Yacob or Ysaac still reeking of the
> Ghetto, snarling a weird Yiddish to the officers of the
> Customs—but had a keener instinct, an intenser energy,
> and a freer hand than he—American of Americans, with
> Heaven knew how many Puritans and Patriots behind
> him, and an education that had cost a civil war.[15]

Self-pity and all, Adams was correct. And that may be as
high a praise of the energy of the American man of his time
as one can offer.

But the dream of power and energy had been knit to the
idea of manhood in America long before the Gilded Age.
The execrable taste; the fusion of monied ostentation with
Darwinian determinism; the strange marriage between sentimentality and rapacity, wealth and morality, culture and
propriety—all deny that the American is the "new man" that
an innocent de Crèvecoeur believed he was one hundred
years earlier. The man who came to the forefront after the

Civil War was dull rather than simple; in him, the frontiers-man's willingness to test his skills against the wilderness now reflected an implacable need to accumulate wealth. His struggle with nature was based on his contempt, for he believed that a strong man had the right to impose his power on anything that stood in his way. When faced with the choice of living harmoniously with the landscape or rooting it up for his own cash interest, the American man did not hesitate for an instant. He might sentimentalize the land, but that was mere hypocrisy.

He still viewed himself as an original, and his belief in his "newness" became a fixed reference point of belief. Irony was not his forte. He did not believe in the inner life but went through the motions of public piety by endowing churches, schools, universities, art galleries. He was still sexually passive, now for a different reason from his forefathers'—his energy had been channelled into making money. And the very kinds of knowledge and pleasure that sex offers, as it probes the self and its needs, are exactly what he has *not* been trained to deal with. Sex cannot be simplified merely by applying more force.

At the time of his greatest explosion of energy, the American man discovered that energy was not enough. The business tycoon approaches sex from a cautious distance, working at it in much the same manner as he spanned the continent with rails or produced cheaper and better steel. His adventures into sensuality have a touchingly comic innocence; he does not so much perform at sex as gawk at it like an adolescent. The locker-room spirit of the thing is a kind of "good old boys" stag party. Here is a description by Howard Mumford Jones of the games invented by powerful men.

At a birthday party for twelve in Diamond Jim's honor, arranged, it is said, by Stanford White in his Hall of Mirrors at the top of the Old Madison Square Garden,

waiters brought in a huge Jack Horner Pie; the guests
were given ribbons and told to pull, the pie opened to
reveal a nude girl, who climbed off the table, sat on
Brady's lap, and fed him dessert. The guests were shortly
favored by the presence of eleven other naked girls.[16]

With a power to buy and sell unmatched in history, the
American man caters to his hidden pubescent fantasies.
There is something uproarious about this, but there is something terribly sad about it, too, as if even in his imagination of
sexuality he cannot get beyond an adolescent dream. The
energy that he has brought to business drains him for sex. As
the nineteenth century draws to a close, sex becomes for
writers and artists a manifestation of a man's courage, the
final frontier to be tamed. Consequently, it is also the final
opportunity for the nation's newest hero, the businessman, to
show his daring. And he fails.

In *The American 1890s*, Larzer Ziff points out that Frank
Norris's businessman hero, Curtis Jadwin, is the very embodiment of what "happens to masculinity in America when the
male's successful pursuit of his role in accordance with the
business ethic drains him of his virility."[17] In novel after
novel, the sexual energy of the American man seems cor-
doned off; virility is to be found in the building of corporate
empires, but even the process of spending money often seems
childish. The rich underground sexuality of Victorian London
finds no match in the New York and Chicago of the 1890s.
What Professor Ziff writes about Norris is essentially true of
the entire culture. "The American businessman . . . excludes
his wife from his characteristically most forceful moments,
leaving her open to seek gratification in lovers, or to pursue
art or social work as substitutes for sexual fulfilment."[18]

Because his position is difficult to maintain, the builder of
railroads and steel mills begins to look at his sexuality more

analytically. He discovers that he must begin to push past the physical and examine his own interior landscape. How prescient Cooper had been when he combined Natty Bumppo's skill as a woodsman and hunter with his fundamental asexuality. But in Natty's flight from women, we can still detect a certain awe of the power of sexuality; his wilderness is at least a metaphorical bride, one that challenges him to face his own fears—as Diamond Jim's party girl never does.

Our own time can look back to both Natty's virginal purity and Diamond Jim's rapacious adolescence from a great distance, at least as far as sex is concerned. And yet, to write this is to acknowledge the fact that the American man is dominated by his sexuality more than he dominates it. So many of the men one meets today seem willing, perhaps even anxious, to get beyond an idea that sex involves making choices. The idea of an independent committed sexuality does not seem to appeal to American men today any more than it did to Deerslayer or to Diamond Jim. Men today have not ceased trying to negate the price expected of their manhood, much as they did in past eras. The naked girl is still popping out of the gigantic pie—only now she is pre-pubescent.

IV

IN THE TWENTIETH CENTURY, American men nurture ideas of what they should be but seem unable to give birth to any new persona they can acknowledge as their own. Manhood seems more and more a series of confused reactions to the very myths it once built upon, a long battle with the necessity of creating coherent structures within which to live. So many of the poems and novels in which the modern man in America speaks to us about himself and his feelings intimate a sense of ruin. In an attempt to purify themselves by confession, men find themselves engulfed only by their numerous dissatisfactions.

No amount of analysis or history can dispel the power of myth. The actuality of what the frontier was like, the reality of the waste of energy and lives that followed the Civil War, such truths were easily overlooked or ignored for the consistencies need created. But the energy of the twentieth century belonged, as Henry Adams had predicted, to the machine rather than to man. And so the mythicization of manhood became even more apparent. It is not that men today actually *believe* in the frontier hero—indeed, our media images, our fictions, even our folklore now serve to temper such myths—but that men want to believe in the forms of manhood such a hero evokes, just as we want to believe that energy embodies strength and potency. We want to believe in order to dispel our sense of loss. The contemporary anti-hero in literature does not struggle with the meaning of his life or the quality of his manhood but with the idea of existence itself. For courage, we have substituted the necessity of dread. And we live within the boundaries that dread inspires.

As the American man emerges from the closed-off landscape of World War II, he experiences a moment of hesitation, of indecision. He has tasted the energy and power with which his fathers and grandfathers had conquered first the frontier and then the world of money. He can sense the strength of his own solid existence among the charred ruins of the 1945 landscape, and emerges as the model for men in Europe—indeed, for men all over the world. He is alive, healthy, envied.

And he is everywhere, signing himself with what becomes the very synonym for his capacity—Kilroy. In the smoking ruins of postwar Europe, Kilroy discovers the landscape from which his fathers moved west. He senses that his manhood can once again be made his own, that the power the centuries have bequeathed him is still, surprisingly enough, *his* power. A new moment of choice: He can remain within this desolation, the one muscular body in the valley of bleached bones, the last true man in the world. Or else he can go home, the civilized normal man his country needs.

The choice is not easy. The complexities of being a man will prove eventful enough; the complexities of being an American may yet prove unbearable. He sniffs the air, smells the smoke of a wrecked Europe, and brings his desire for responsibility and peace back to America. He has accepted the necessity of changing the world; he has shown that he is not afraid, that he is still a man in whom courage is a critical obligation.

What else is Kilroy? However wry the humor, however mocking his presence in his very desire to leave the complexities of death and Europe and return to the small-town Midwestern bosom, Kilroy is fate's commentary upon the sheer absurdity of being a child of the frontier in the middle of the twentieth century. He is a parody of the very self he embodies, instinctively recognizing the inherent humor of being an American in this foreign Europe. *"Amerika, du hast es besser."* Kilroy smiles, puzzled, a bit self-conscious, and holds onto his singular manhood. The men he sees in Europe are prisoners in their own lands, devoid of sustaining myths, the very image of what he himself fears. The worst threat to his own life would be if he proved unable to control his own destiny. And so he wants to leave Europe, to feel his own power, his presence as a man.

Men now in their fifties and sixties look back to their service days during the Second World War with nostalgia and envy, and this is no accident. In their voices there is a note of lament for that which has been transformed into the best of times simply by having been the worst that they had come through. It is easy to belittle this as a simple manifestation of the Archie Bunker syndrome—for Archie is the man who fought in "WW II, the big one." But to do this is to be incredibly shortsighted. For the true myth here is the omnipresent Kilroy. He was there, he who embodies the American man at the last moment in his history when the American could rely on his unambiguous sense of his own manhood and feel no need to justify it or himself. Ambivalence has not yet overwhelmed him. He has asserted his presence by taking part in a collective effort that demanded specific skills. Of course, European men had been fighting even longer, and undoubtedly with equal skill, determination, and courage. But Kilroy sees himself as unique, a true citizen, aware of the responsibilities he must meet. His job now is to rescue the world from itself, to Americanize Europe. Kilroy is there, he is here, he is everywhere.

But when he returns to America he discovers that the "new man" has finally died in that very Europe which gave him birth. He is now only a cautious hero for a frightened time, no longer an outlaw—at best, he is a misfit, a bumbling citizen trying to meet all the obligations that have been thrust upon him. He refuses risk. While he records his presence on latrine walls and across the ruined palaces of Europe, he dreams of a small house in a small town in Ohio, a front yard with a white climber of red roses kept neat by a wife who looks like June Allyson. And children. And a good, steady job. And a clean, modern landscape sectioned off into neat, functional compartments.

The wilderness has ended. Deerslayer is no longer a dream, simply a figure about whom academics write. He was never meant to be father and husband and to live in a small town in Ohio. The promise of Kilroy's wartime European dreams was greater somehow. Had he not promised himself he would impose his reality on the world as he left his signature here and there and everywhere? He looks around. His wife is still pretty; his children have grown; he has his house, a larger one now, with the front yard and the climber of red roses.

Every three years there is a new car in the garage, a sense of possession, of solidity, to enforce his sense of security. His achievements are distinct, measurable, substantial. Better this than sweating it out in stinking outhouses or running through Europe trying to save all those relics of a life that has been left to molder.

Still, he is dissatisfied, uncomfortable, exhausted. One by one, the possibilities seem to have passed him by. He has been sucked into the business of living, husband-father-provider-soldier-in-the-ranks. Doctor, lawyer, Indian chief. He feels himself judged and, strangely enough, he believes that he has been found wanting. He discovers that he envies Deerslayer both his freedom and his doom as a virginal lover, always hovering on the edge of his own sureties. But now there are no more forests to penetrate and master. This flat Midwestern landscape maps out a series of dead ends. Older and heavier and increasingly depressed and angry, Kilroy stands on his front lawn and curses the graffiti of America's own inner exiles. A miasma of purposelessness seizes him; he drifts toward a dull paranoia. Kilroy senses that he has been robbed of his legitimacy, his birthright as an American man. The past that he knew only as a surface on which to speed toward his own manhood has now slipped away. In the chaos of Europe, he had at least stood with his own. But now he is alone, unable to join hands with the other Kilroys, each of them standing on his own lawn in his own anger and confusion. Each looks back to the war, trying to remember that time when worst was best.

As he remembers what he was, Kilroy senses that men are rarely better than the myths that give them form. He sees his neighbor grow his hair long, run away with his secretary, leave his wife and his three high-school-aged children. And Kilroy is disgusted, angered at his own image. He acknowledges how much of a homeboy he was, is, will forever be. And then he looks into his neighbor's empty lawn and discovers that he can no longer reconcile his role as a man with what he actually is. A sense of turbulent amazement seizes him. He is afraid.

All around him he hears voices urging him on toward newer, greater proofs of the self's capacity. He is told to become a sexual outlaw; he is urged to drop the stress and strain and fold himself, a naked shimmering ego, into the drug-drenched quiescence he yearns for; he is told to become as cunning as a wolf on the prowl in a world where technological heroism can be his, too; he is told to lie in bed and chain himself to his own illusions, his none-too-subtle fantasies. Television, discos, massage parlors—all promise him the revolution he never even knew he wanted.

And when he looks for help to the writers and artists and myth-makers, he discovers that the shaping power of their imagination is limited by the same confusion he feels. Kilroy stands alone. And his manhood, once the gift of his passage through life, is now shrunken, dwarfed, devalued. Hemingway, Miller, Mailer, Bellow, Updike, all have recognized this and have sought to reclaim its lost vitality. And all have failed.

As the sense of manhood withers, the fictional worlds men inhabit are fleshed out. Bodies kiss bodies, art walks hand in hand with pornography, each seeking a style the masculine will can call its own. But the dead Deerslayer cannot be revived. A note of elegy sounds in the harsh desperation with which writers now describe American men. For Kilroy, they have discovered, is here, thinking about the sons he has sent forth, remembering how they have turned on his dreams and inverted his nightmares. Deerslayer molders beneath the forest, the frozen leaves pile high on the land. And from the throat of each Kilroy standing alone on his lawn comes the cry, "I want!"

FOOTNOTES

1. R. W. B. Lewis, *The American Adam: Innocence, Tragedy, and Tradition in the Nineteenth Century* (Chicago, 1955), p. 5. In a book dealing with manhood in America, I discover that I have found more of value in literary criticism and cultural history than I have in the social sciences. Along with Lewis's *The American Adam*, I am particularly indebted to Henry Nash Smith's *Virgin Land: The American West as Symbol and Myth* and Richard Slotkin's *Regeneration Through Violence: The Mythology of the American Frontier, 1600–1860.*

2. Frederick Jackson Turner's "The Significance of the Frontier in American History" was a brilliant outline of the effect of the frontier on the development of American character. Delivered as a paper at a meeting of the American Historical Association in 1893, the Turner Thesis has passed from a historical idea intended to explain the peculiarities of American development into a metaphor which addresses itself to the particulars of American character. As a metaphor, it has demonstrated far more staying power than it commanded as a historical thesis. No theory can "explain" the American man, but because metaphor and cultural myth are so closely related, Turner's thesis seems to me a welcome addition to any attempt to deal with what we expect of manhood here in America.

3. Hector St. John de Crèvecoeur, *Letters from an American Farmer* (New York, 1912), p. 60.

4. Benjamin Franklin, *Autobiography* (New York, 1969), p. 80.

5. Henry Nash Smith, *Virgin Land* (New York, 1950), p. 114. The persona was so powerful that the cultural myth it created defied both reality and caricature. It is almost impossible to restore a true historical perspective by showing us the cowboy or the frontiersman as he really was. Both the western novel and the western film mythicize that manhood by melding character to landscape. Even a fine novel such as Walter Van Tilburg Clark's *The Ox-Bow Incident,* which was made into one of the best American films, ultimately

seems to endorse the toughness and the willingness to face truth
that the American man must recognize. And yet, both novel and
film are attacks upon the idea of American individualism, an individualism which is viewed as leading to the herd instinct.

6. See Leslie Fiedler's *Love and Death in the American Novel* (New
York, 1962)—particularly the chapter entitled "James Fenimore
Cooper and the Historical Romance."

7. Throughout the nineteenth century, foreign observers comment
upon the American's blindness about himself. More often than not,
the individual they are speaking about is the American man. The
writings of de Tocqueville, Mrs. Martineau, Mrs. Trollope, and
Captain Hall, even when they are motivated by a certain sympathy
for Americans, evoke pictures of a manhood which often border on
caricature. And even if we cannot trust the objectivity of the young
nation's British and French visitors, that is no reason for not trust-
ing their sight.

8. "Crockett's Brag," *American Literature: The Makers and the
Making*, Vol. I, ed. Cleanth Brooks, R. W. B. Lewis, and Robert Penn
Warren (New York, 1973), pp. 1097–98.

9. David Riesman, with Nathan Glazer and Reuel Denney, *The
Lonely Crowd: A Study of the Changing American Character*,
abridged edition (New York, 1956), p. 35.

10. For the past twenty years, the study of the cultural and psycho-
logical changes generated by the Civil War has resulted in a number
of outstanding books. Four that I found of particular interest were
Daniel Aaron's *The Unwritten War*, George M. Frederickson's *The
Inner Civil War*, William R. Taylor's *Cavalier and Yankee*, and
Edmund Wilson's *Patriotic Gore*.

11. Henry Adams, *The Education of Henry Adams* (Boston, 1961),
p. 417. The phrase is used to describe Teddy Roosevelt.

12. Howard Mumford Jones, *The Age of Energy: Varieties of American Experience, 1865–1915* (New York, 1970), pp. 136–37. Professor Jones, in this excellent cultural inquiry into the period
between the Civil War and the First World War, defines energy in

the Gilded Age as being "both amoral and ambiguous." It is interesting to note that where the American man was usually accused of an excess of energy, the accusation made against him today is increasingly of a want of energy. A good deal of the rhetoric calling for spontaneity and freedom also demands, if only by implication, a view of energy as that which drains men and dehumanizes them. See Philip Slater's *The Pursuit of Loneliness* and see also William Irwin Thompson's *At the Edge of History: Speculations on the Transformation of Culture.*

13. Adams, p. 265.

14. Edmund Wilson, *Patriotic Gore: Studies in the Literature of the American Civil War* (New York, 1962), p. 133.

15. Adams, p. 238.

16. Jones, p. 126.

17. Larzer Ziff, *The American 1890s: Life and Times of a Lost Generation* (New York, 1966), p. 273. "Jadwin is a bull in the market," Ziff notes, "in the vocabulary of finance, but Norris also makes it clear that the bull who rushes about all day goring and dodging in the pit on La Salle Street returns home at night having spilled his vital seed. He is less than his virile self in his marital relations. . . ."

18. Ibid, p. 273. There are, of course, exceptions. If the businessmen of Howells and James and Norris seem sexually inadequate, Dreiser's Frank Cowperwood is as accumulative and hard-driving in his sexual pursuits as he is in his relentless take-over of the Chicago transportation system.

Chapter Four
Hemingway's Pain

It takes a pretty good man to make any sense when he's dying.

—Hemingway to Lillian Ross

I

WE CREATE OUR OWN METAPHORS for disease. But death is subtler, a more limited possession. Death denies the power of metaphor. Its very simplicity refuses the bromides with which we try to distort it. The threat of death is the threat of ultimate excess. Its residual impact is measured not by the life that has been lost but from the effect of that life on those who remember it, who try to graft it onto their own lives, who continue to try to make sense of it. Disease claims a territory, embeds itself in the mind's geography. But death denies geography, compresses an entire existence into an object to be held up for other people's judgement. "Death only closes a man's reputation," wrote Addison in *The Spectator,* "and determines it as good or bad." The living are the ones who have an investment in death, for it is they who are finally left with the problem of what to make of the life that has ended.

The living seize the dead and ventilate their lives, invading every private alley to find those moments in which lives merge in the condition of being a man. And yet, the deaths we examine are not those known immediately to us; rather, they are the deaths of our symbolic fathers. For we all wanted more than the biological father. We scoured the world for usable fathers-by-adoption, insisting that they serve as models. And so many of us, even those who are tempted to deny the quest today, found that father in Hemingway.

I did not know that I was typical in what I sought from Hemingway, for neither the paradoxes of my own life nor the pretensions of his were fully available to me then. But I knew that when I looked at what surrounded me, a world of immigrants in which the kind of manhood America demanded was kept at a distance, I wanted something else. Down all the crooked corridors of my mind, I would search for other fantasies, other models after whom to pattern my own existence. And yet, mine was a cautious search. I kept myself aware of the distinctions between real and unreal. I might have envied that body looming gigantically before me on my Saturday afternoon excursions into darkened movie theaters, but once I stepped outside I knew enough to leave such fantasies where they belonged. For the children of immigrants were perceptive enough to understand that life demanded a strict accounting. The process of growing toward manhood could not be allowed to become too sentimental. Nor could it be allowed to appear demonic. What we could not get from our fathers was what we took from our fathers-by-adoption: the idea that manhood was a natural process, that in seizing the opportunities open to us we were establishing ourselves as men and as Americans—a most potent combination. Manhood reflected those distinct portions of existence that we read about in the actual lives of the men we admired. We did not literally want to become what other men appeared to be. But reading about their lives made us probe our own possibilities of becoming the men we thought we might become. We sought subaltern fathers in the hope that their very presence in the world would *sponsor* our emergence into the manhood we wanted.

It is difficult to explain why so many of us thought we had found our man in Hemingway. But it was in him, a writer who seemed to assert his independence of the common life at the very same time that he spoke for it, that I and so many of my contemporaries discovered the country's mirror of what it expected of us. At this point in time, when we have to look closely at the choices we made, the very strain of our existence is fused to the inadequacy of his. No one could quite measure up to what we needed—not, god knows, a man scourging himself in public for the very qualities we wanted him to demonstrate. And so we turned against that which had not proven adequate to our needs—and we turned, convinced that what was at stake was the culture's ability to see itself as valid, not the validity of the hero. We felt obliged to reduce in stature, if not altogether destroy, those fathers we had adopted, and this was not merely the revolt of one generation against a predecessor. It was, I believe, a revolt against our recognition that the manhood we sought did not finally exist independent of all else. No matter what Hemingway's actual achievement, it was not quite enough for our needs. Perhaps that fate had been guaranteed from the very beginning. To become a father-by-adoption was to be pushed aside, as the biological father was pushed aside, when the son discovered that the time for revolt had arrived.

Looking back, I can see that what I wanted from Hemingway was probably beyond his power, indeed, beyond the power of any writer, to offer. I would eventually have to turn against the massive contradictions his idea of manhood inspired, aware that I was cutting myself off from a life that I had once viewed as typical in its aspirations and demands. At seventeen, however, when I first read Hemingway, I needed a certain literalness for my own existence, and I sought from him an approach to manhood in which those attitudes he had made so meaningful in his fiction might prove to be a basis on which I could build my own ability to endure in adversity. Although the quality of the endurance he offered is far more distant today, I still owe the man an obligation. For more than any other writer, it was Hemingway who first made me aware of the relationship between endurance and manhood.

Hemingway, for me, was the embodiment of the very possibility of becoming a man. The tenor of his existence was what I tried to catch when I read his fiction—and soon I was trying to catch it in the gossipy snippets about him that I read in Leonard Lyons or Walter Winchell. There were no other figures who seemed so attractive. In no other writer of our country, perhaps in no other man, had America embedded the actual presence of manhood as it had in Ernest Hemingway. That alone should have told us that we would eventually have to un-make the man, to pull him apart like a discarded rag doll. If I—and so many other American men who tried to use his life as an example—were to turn on him so harshly, that was because the task I had set for him was impossible. I had more difficulty in facing that fact than he could ever have. His task, I had assumed, was to teach me how to be a man, not to entertain me, not even to show me as writers have always shown the young. No, just as I went to school to prepare myself for a career, so I read Hemingway in order to learn to be an American man.

It is a cliché by now to acknowledge that Hemingway is no longer fashionable. And the extent of that unfashionability can be seen in the periodic attempts to rescue his literary reputation by remaking his life. More than anyone else in twentieth-century America, he is a writer in whom art and life blend. It has become even more difficult to speak of the one without the other since his suicide. No wonder we find the figure he has become increasingly awkward and difficult to handle. For we discover that we treat the man even more than we treat the man's work. And so we are forever caught trying to cleanse him of what we see as a sophomoric view of existence.[1]

Even those who asked him to serve as a model are bound to find him embarrassing, often even boring, if they reread him without the youthful expectations his work inspired. In part, the fault for this lies not with Hemingway nor with that famous style he brought to literature. It lies more with the memory of one's own need to be the man he thought Hemingway had mapped out. In 1950, when I first read him, Hemingway's was a voice I could confidently adopt as model—part precursor, part prophet, a man whose writing resonated with those specific kinds of experience which promised to separate me from the fate that might conceivably be mine. He urged me on, insisting that even if the tragedy of life was inevitable, the styles with which one approached that tragedy were the very stuff of meaning. Even then, I suppose I suspected that both his experience and his prose had been frozen in a posturing that bordered on the ludicrous. And yet, I continued to focus on what the man demanded and how the writer behaved. It would have been easier to handle had Hemingway been simply one more writer rather than a writer who was my image of what a man could be. I once shared this problem with a friend of mine, also seventeen, who nodded and said, "You come right down to it, not even Hemingway can be Hemingway." Perhaps not. But he could try and we could imitate the attempt.

Hemingway was a public figure, a man whose every gesture had the same journalistic currency as the gestures of a Hollywood film star. Because of this, payment for his art demanded a massive public relations campaign for his life. Ultimately, he became too public, too successful in his pursuit of the worship we were willing to give him. The great white hunter, the journalist who was a better soldier than the men he covered, the world traveller, the boxing fan and race horse tout—all seemed to combine into a man who simply left too many debts in his wake. By the time he died, he seemed worn out, a parody of the very man we had once thought he was. But even here, we felt he stood for something. For if we faced the limitations of his manhood, then we might yet delude ourselves into believing that we did not have to face the limitations of our own.

Long before his death, the reputation of Hemingway the

writer had begun to wane, his talent increasingly obscured by the thickening self-consciousness of Hemingway the man, the image-maker caught in one of his numerous poses. In actual fact, the critical assault on his work coincides with his emergence as a writer in the 1920s. From the very beginning, it was his personality, specifically his projection of a self-involved manhood, that became the focus of critical perception. He made *himself* an issue, and was the first American writer to do this successfully. He became a *poète maudit,* a man who conceived of his own existence on a gargantuan scale. He thrust his presence before the world with all the self-conscious "toughness" of a ten-year-old challenging his peers to knock the chip off his shoulder. His ambitions were ferocious—think of the disguises and counter-disguises the man had to create and then learn to live with. He was hunter and intellectual, literary stylist and fighter, supreme publicist for the self and man of few words, Catholic and hedonist. Even in *A Moveable Feast,* his posthumously published book about his early years in Paris, the purpose is to claim a verifiable manhood, to settle accounts with a world of "enemies." There is something dreadfully childish about this book—and that despite the fact that it contains as fine a prose as Hemingway had written since those early years in Paris. The man we meet here scoring points off the dead bodies of Ford Madox Ford and Gertrude Stein and F. Scott Fitzgerald has carefully sealed off his real past. He is "getting his own back," creating portrait after portrait in which memory rejects true intimacy for vengeance. *A Moveable Feast* sweeps the past clean of obstacles that threaten Hemingway the man. Fearful of the sense of failure he must have acknowledged toward the end of his life, he withdrew into the hard core of the American manhood he had so consciously, so meticulously, fashioned. A man. An American man. For many of us, *the* American man. And a man who moves relentlessly towards his own self-destruction, still intent on justifying his manhood, or else be damned in the attempt. *A Moveable Feast* is a memoir filled with ambushes of all those enemies Hemingway suspected were lying in wait to ambush his own supreme creation, his manhood. Lesbians, homosexuals, aesthetes, literary hangers-on—all threaten him, all interfere with the writer's dedication to craft, to truth, and to his manly self. Blindly shuttered in his paranoid isolation, hearing the venemous whispers, the gloom seems to have spread through every fiber of his being. How terrible the price— moving toward death, still needing to prove your manhood, to yourself, to those around you, and to the lingering ghosts. And how relentlessly American.

For Hemingway, the need to prove his manhood was virtually conterminous with the craft he forged. However famous his literary style became, it was carefully kept subservient to the man's need to proclaim the specific qualities of his manhood—hunter, fisherman, soldier, boxer, the hero who is capable of living within the conscious immediacies of his own death.

For death is always in the forefront for the writer. With Hemingway in particular, death was the focus of manhood. If a man's prowess was to be demonstrated by the ways in which he defied the limits of his own mortality, then only a developed consciousness of death might offer the background against which he could test his capacities legitimately. No writer was more intent on forcing his consciousness of death to the surface.[2] In his work, as in his life, death is fundamental—defining suffering, relieving boredom, offering a way out. Death was not merely a rite of passage for Hemingway; it was the chief possibility a man could face when he placed his body in physical danger, when he was forced to measure its ruin against its promise. Consciousness of death blended his life and art; it was at the center of everything he wrote. Even more important, it formed the core of his manhood, enabling him to match his resistance against its inevitable demands.

And it was, finally, what separated the man who was conscious of his need to be a man from his peers.

There is legitimate reason to criticize Hemingway. Faulkner was the more highly endowed writer, Fitzgerald responded more honestly to the complexities of American life, both Dreiser and Farrell understood the taut lines of class in this country and how they work in ways that would have been inconceivable for Hemingway. One can admit that the work is limited, the man embarrassing. And yet, having admitted all this, there remains the enduring fascination of Hemingway, particularly if we want to understand the price demanded of manhood in America. This is why Hemingway's life is written about so often, for it is a life that promises to reveal so much about what we ourselves are. His life remains his supreme fiction, his legacy of the power and assertion that he put into being a man. Not that his life is a lie. It is, rather, a creation, and as he parades it before us, sometimes subtly, sometimes pompously, sometimes furtively, we suspect that he has encased his manhood in the trappings America had offered him.

In retrospect, the public bravado, the pictures in *Esquire* of Hemingway standing above animals he had killed in Africa, the obsequious quotations of gossip columnists which showed up more and more as the talent withered to less and less—all of this compresses into a small gesture of defiance, like graffiti on subway cars. The attention-getters are embarrassing and unattractive and they are real and they are, finally, necessary to establish the quality of Hemingway's achievement *into* manhood. As much as anything else one can name, it was his manhood-posing that explains the usual charge levelled against him—that he was an adolescent. But this adolescence frightens us *because* it incorporates itself into the structure of manhood. And our scorn for it may speak more of the contemporary failure to accept manhood as a challenge to the individual, something that has to be reached for and taken, than it does of Hemingway's shortcomings. For Hemingway showed us, as few writers actually manage to do, how important it is that we recognize the truths the adolescent confronts as he tests himself. Hemingway understood that boys looked forward to the condition of manhood primarily because it was presented to them as something which one needed courage to take. He understood that the soul, like the face it mirrors, breaks out in its own acne—and that the soul's acne can never be eliminated, merely masked.

His life does not serve our needs today. In the current drift toward a unisex culture, Hemingway has been demoted to being one of the enemy. But in the future, after our gender battles have quieted down, we may again be able to put him to use. He may, after all, be able to help us approach one of the problems we are probably never going to be rid of— exactly what it is we mean by manhood. For the idea of manhood will not disappear into an androgynous ether. We are still going to have to face that male adolescent as he asks how he can get beyond narcissism and yet accept the challenges the world has in store for him. And we may also, in the process, discover that our problems with sexual definition remain, that the world is still filled with men and women who are conscious of being either men or women. It is well to remember why Hemingway once had so much appeal to those on the edge of manhood: He could seize hold of one's coming of age in America, and he could illuminate the hesitant beginnings and false starts of becoming a man.

II

HEMINGWAY'S LIFE WAS SIMPLE ENOUGH; his complexity emerges from what he felt he had to create out of that life.[3] He obstinately refused to permit experience to pass him by.

Still, he exhibited a distant caution, approaching us like a man inching his way forward, searching for unknown dangers. No matter how rebellious he might have wanted to seem, his life is stained by a solid sense of propriety. It is as if, in becoming the Hemingway of legend, he had deliberately set out to make his life a traditional American success story by inverting middle-class morality. In many respects, he kept the highly conservative and controlled life his doctor-father bequeathed him. Given the tone of his Midwestern past, the conservatism was inevitable, and this was not merely a conservatism of style. No, he was a writer for whom limitation and measurement ultimately coincided. What he did best was what he controlled most carefully. And the control he exerted over his writing was equally apparent in the construction of his life and the projection of his image. He was not a true rebel; he was not even really rebellious. The limitations of his prose are apparent in his life.

Today, even his suicide seems inevitable, given the man's measured response to life. "The eye of every dream Hemingway had must have looked down the long vista of his future suicide—so he had a legitimate fear of chaos," writes Mailer.[4] Suicide was the only choice still available, the final way in which he could impose meaning on his life. He was obviously desperate, battered beyond endurance, but suicide now seems a lead he took from his father, just as he took so much else, obeying him and challenging him at one and the same time. As he had earlier obeyed and challenged him in hunting and fishing, or, more subtly, in living with a solid bourgeois sense of obligation, so he now did in the matter of life and death. Sons do not get away so easily in America.

His own suicide must have sounded a strangely redemptive note for him that moment before he pulled the trigger. But for the rest of us the redemption proves too expensive, as if suicide were the ultimate chip to be knocked off the shoulder.

"At a certain point of despair," writes Anthony Alvarez, "a man will kill himself in order to show he is serious."[5] In Hemingway's case, this point was reached when the excess of pain threatened to turn consciousness itself into a hollow white light behind which the self saw not its death but its complete disintegration. The obligation to endure pain struggled with the need to take one's leave with some dignity intact. Both the endurance of the pain and the maintenance of dignity depended upon the conviction that the choice of suicide represented the culmination of a battle.

Hemingway possessed a traditionally Western view of suicide. His ultimate solution to the disintegration that he saw in his own life must have come down to a choice between humiliations. Of course, it is impossible to know this for sure, but the supposition has the man's life behind it. He had long been on the side of those for whom suicide represented negation, surrender, an action in which a man sheds his courageous self and gives in to cowardice. Even if the despair of the suicide lent it authenticity, it was no less cowardly (at least that was his reaction to the suicide of his own father). And what was true of the doctor turned out to be true of the doctor's son. Committing suicide was giving up on his own manhood, admitting the inadequacy of what he had spoken of as "grace under pressure." And grace under pressure, the reader of Hemingway senses, was a specifically masculine grace, to be fought for and possessed if one was to be a man. It is a curious phrase, and it strikes an additional adolescent note. Grace under pressure, according to Hemingway, is the kind of courage which pits itself against the world and which seeks to measure manliness through the ability to accept adversity.[6]

Ultimately, his was an adolescent's attitude toward suicide. But if Hemingway was an adolescent, as charged, he was a great adolescent. His world was consistently uncertain, filled

with tests. The possession of grace under pressure is fleeting;
it lacks permanence, solidity. A man's moment of triumph
carries no assurances for his future, except that he is going to
have to struggle once again to maintain that grace. Even to
speak about it is to run the risk of loss, to find that
it has disappeared, leaving him raging and impotent in its
wake. It is adolescent to believe that whenever temptation
arrives, betrayal threatens, that judgement is inevitable. For
Hemingway, it was also true.

III

HE WAS MOST ADOLESCENT of all in the ways in which he
understood pain. For pain provides meaning, and constitutes
a connection between the individual and his world. And it is
exactly here, in the ability to endure pain, that performance
is so frequently tested. Hemingway understood this; it was as
profound a truth as he ever seized upon. It was not pain itself
that fascinated him but the confrontation of the particular
self with a specific amount of pain. Pointing out the connection was one of the lessons he managed to show others. It was
certainly one he showed me, and I have never ceased to be
grateful to him for it. The qualities he insisted a man demonstrate were exactly those I needed in my own struggle with
what the virus had done to me. In a book I wrote years ago, I
spoke of him as "my nurse." He soothed my fears, helped me
transform incapacity into capacity, helped me meet those
challenges to my existence which insisted that I was incapa-
ble of defining myself. No writer has ever given me more.
However awkward this may sound, I wanted to make myself
the kind of American man who would manage to win approval in his eyes. What I wanted him to teach me was how to
set about creating myself, my inner man. And who knew

more about manhood or the endurance it demanded than Hemingway?

The endurance of pain was the key to the gifts he offered. I remember, soon after I began to read Hemingway, walking mile after mile with my crutches literally eating into the pits of my shoulders, thinking that I was somehow going to gain the approval of a man who did not even know of my existence and who would, no doubt, have been puzzled if not openly appalled at the role which I insisted he accept. I needed to make myself over, to repair my body, so that I could reach into manhood. And to the extent that pain affirmed my need, to the extent that the endurance of pain could testify to how I had met the challenge of transforming myself, to that extent I welcomed the pain. And the Hemingway I had created in my mind was both solicitous and judgemental. To map out my own pain meant that I had come through. This may be what Becker means when he speaks of how pain "calls the body to the forefront of existence."[7] For I was aware—and it was Hemingway who helped make me aware—that pain spoke of *my* ability, *my* endurance, and finally *my* sense of manhood that I was advancing against the world.

Hemingway taught me a way in which to use pain. Later, I recognized that his work also provided me with the example of a personal style, a way of confronting the demands American life made upon men. For me, Hemingway's major perception was that the demands pain made upon the body were legitimate. He understood the difference between pain as a form of humiliation and pain as the promise for future redemption. Any male adolescent would vigorously pursue that promise, for it affirms his sense of his own existence. In forcing us to recognize what pain demanded of the body, Hemingway made it possible to understand that pain was a test and that it promised a singular presence, a self that, whatever its limitations, was identifiably *yours*. Pain heightens sensation; it makes the body know that it is alive, that it has a chance to endure: not, of course, pain that is so great as to blind a man to other sensations but pain that permits him to extend his capacity.

The kind of courage Hemingway struggled to possess is not particularly fashionable any longer, but the body possesses its own record, its own obligations. Like most adolescents, Hemingway expected an inordinate amount from his own body. He was, apparently, not particularly well coordinated, and yet he insisted on punishing that body down through the years. His lifelong predilection for accidents is suspicious; his numerous broken bones, his wounds, his frequent courting of death, his insistence on a first-rate physical performance—all speak of a man struggling to meet the challenges his rigorous adolescent structures have created. He was able to beat his body's protests down in a way that testifies to the adolescent's dream of prowess. In Hemingway's fiction, pain is never distinctly sexual but it can be sensual. Unlike the sadist, who views pain as an invariable concomitant of pleasure—the very heart of pleasure—Hemingway keeps it at a distance. It is the price a man must pay for control, a test in which the capacity to take it, to absorb pain that is meaningful, is paramount.

And in Hemingway's writing, the body possesses a distinct life of its own. His own body betrayed him—he could not reach the goals he set for it: It broke down of its own internal contradictions. The man was always being patched and mended. Perhaps because of this, his body created his subject matter as much as his mind had. Pain was his thesis; the body offered to create an antithesis with which he might withstand the threat of pain as humiliation.

The many photographs of him show a man who, until the last ten years of his life at least, might have served as the physical model for Fitzgerald's Tom Buchanan in *The Great Gatsby*. His is an American body, a Midwestern body, a "cruel body"—but a body that manifests its presence, its very physicality set in opposition to what the world can do to it. It is a big body, one that expresses the nuances of a man's character; it rolls back into itself and it seems tight, controlled, powerful, physically responsive to the need to maintain its own dignity. It is a body that insists that it is capable of enduring pain. And in Hemingway the endurance of pain is always a kind of dignity, while the loss of dignity is what the individual must constantly struggle against. Like the imagination, the body is condemned to express itself. Fishing, hunting, skiing—these are not sports in Hemingway's work but states of being. Much of the action of his best fiction is filtered through the demands his protagonists make on their bodies. And it is fair to add that, on a certain level, Hemingway's body overwhelmed his existence as a writer—and the first to feel its heaviness was Hemingway himself.

Pain not only brings the body into heightened awareness, it also testifies to each man's ultimate failure. Inevitably, there are limits to endurance. Here, too, Hemingway's groping for a usable position is adolescent. He conceived of courage as the ability to live with pain. Pain might at times be liberating, and one did not have to be a masochist to accept this. To endure physical pain without surrendering to one's own limitations is, of course, fundamental to the male adolescent. Such pride is a fence between him and the world. The ways in which he measures prowess are not the ways of middle-class society. He knows that one of his greatest problems is declaring his limits. And he can never be assured that he possesses the endurance he needs. Hemingway best states this theme in that most bloated of his books, *Death in the Afternoon:* "Courage comes from such a short distance; from the heart to the head; but when it goes no one knows how far away it goes."

And yet, even courage could be overwhelmed by the need to win approval, a need apparent in all public men. His own complexity was always catching him unawares. Even in those personal encounters he orchestrated, Hemingway appears to

have been an unusually sneaky fighter. He cast off the traditional Protestant virtue of "fair play" in an attempt to adopt
the ethics of a street fighter. There is a certain lack of integrity here; his famous fights with Morley Callaghan and Max
Eastman are reflections of this. Even more revealing is a
curious incident that occurred in 1942, when the Brooklyn
Dodgers baseball team trained in Havana, where Hemingway
lived. Billy Herman, the Dodgers second baseman, recalls
that Hemingway came down to training camp and invited
four of the players—Herman, Larry French, Augie Galan, and
Hugh Casey—to accompany him to a Havana gun club and
then to his house. He insisted that they drink and eat with
him, and he gave each of them an autographed copy of *For
Whom the Bell Tolls*. Quite suddenly, he challenged Casey to
a fight. "As Hugh was putting his gloves on," Herman recalls,
"Hemingway suddenly hauls off and belted him." Casey then
knocked Hemingway down repeatedly, until Hemingway
"kicked Casey in the balls." Hemingway then insisted that
Casey return the next day to fight a duel. "And he's dead
serious about it," insists Herman. "He wanted to kill Casey.
Hughie'd got the better of him, and Hemingway wanted to
kill him."[8]

IV

EVEN SO, THE MAN LINGERS IN MEMORY. He was, after all, a
presence, and despite his limitations he gave a great deal. It is
difficult for anyone to make a final statement about this father-by-adoption, to absorb the ways in which his life and
work seem set in opposition to one another and are then fused
together. It is even difficult to speak about his personality;
after all, modern writers offer us a series of personas rather
than personalities. And these personas come in layers, each

one peeling off to show what lies beneath, creating an illusion that changes with each passing moment.

In reading about Hemingway, we rarely feel that we have touched the actual man himself. We know that he was not a particularly attractive human being, that he could never overcome the ravages of his own ego. But even if there *were* an absolutely reliable version of the man's life, it would not really prove adequate as the biography of an adopted father. In the long run, what counts is what that life continues to mean to me and to others of my generation, as well as what it may once again come to mean in the future. No matter how much we may berate ourselves for misplaced loyalties, no matter how often we may protest the man's failure to be the person who could fill our need, no matter how annoyed we may grow with our desire for fathers whom we can emulate, Hemingway's life continues to create its own importance. For Hemingway remains an American paradigm. A man. *Our* man. It is not his skill as a writer that we have to come to terms with. Nor is it his mind, nor his emotional insights, nor his personal complexity (although he was undoubtedly far more complex than the tough-guy pose he felt obligated to assume).

We have to come to terms with the fact that he set himself up as an authority on virtues which are pressing in the life of any American man. One need only look at the themes his life and work attempted to unify—manhood as a response to the challenges that lie so thick in the American air; the necessity of courage and endurance and the fear of speaking about those necessities; the ability to use pain to reify a man's very existence. Our world today seems to find the virtues he claimed distant, even quaint. Still, the experience of questing after these virtues remains real. No matter how limited Hemingway himself may seem today, even if we admit that he was often vicious, small-minded, parochial, sometimes even dull-witted, his example still is worth speaking about.

For Hemingway pointed toward the necessity to be a man.
And though he himself failed in that very pursuit, he at least
understood its inevitability. At eighteen, I read Joyce for his
sense of language and Faulkner for his style and Eliot for the
middle-aged desperation I had already learned to call "our
situation." But I needed more than this. And so I read Hemingway as I sensed I must—to learn how to live and to see
whether, having been broken in body by disease, I might still
be as good a man as I thought I had a chance to be. That was
the rich side of adolescence, the knowledge that all involvement is personal. My debt to Hemingway resides, finally, in
what I learned a man could make out of his own life. That
Hemingway himself is the ultimately pathetic victim of the
very virtues he stood for is beside the point. For if it is finally
true that not even Hemingway could be Hemingway, he still
could struggle to be the man his talent and imagination had
created. And I could try to emulate what I thought he ap-
proved. At seventeen, it forced me to confront the man I
could be.

V

How, THEN, DO WE NOW ABSORB the specific failures of the
man's life? His failure to live up to the myths his life and
work seemed to call for is difficult to explain away. We cannot rescue the man from himself. And we are aware that he
never really approached the standards he set for himself. He
was, apparently, a poor father; like any celebrity, he is open
to suspicion as a lover and husband; he was ravaged by the
exhaustion of energies he insisted were singular. Even when
we look at the literary scene, there are better examples of
manhood: Orwell's cranky desperation embodies a deeper
courage than Hemingway possessed, the consistency of
Camus's obligations a braver manner of meeting the world.

But in neither of these writers could the failure have been as personal, for in neither of them was the example of manhood as personal.

I doubt whether those searching for a father-by-adoption today would still choose Hemingway. He is, it turns out, one of our losers. After courage has been served at the table, the other dishes prove inadequate, like Hemingway himself. He tried to make the self indistinguishable from the world that self had created, but it didn't work—not for the writer, not for the man. The shortcomings of the characters he invented pull and scratch at him. They are all attitudes, poses, heavy wooden statues carved by a sculptor for whom mass must disguise a lack of individuation. The phrases about courage begin to parody themselves, just as the characters and settings of the later books parody the young master.

Adopted fathers die, too. And their deaths can be more terrible than the deaths of our real fathers, for we can see our better selves in the man who has gone under. The legitimate chaos that any man must feel as he ages was transformed in Hemingway into one more attempt at self-promotion. If only near the end he had been able to seize hold of his own very fragmentary being and stand on that brittle edge where proving one's manhood is the self's true desperation. And not a quiet desperation at that, but one that could send a man baying at the moon. For the manhood trial, as Hemingway knew, is never over, never complete, and manhood itself is never really won. Hemingway might have written brilliantly about that. Having transformed himself into an advertisement for the ambitions of manhood even as his talent dwindled, he might, near the end, have written a novel so naked in its judgement and so absolute in the quality of its desperation that it would have stunned even those who had never believed in his style of manhood. Instead, he tried to disguise his vulnerability, to refuse to admit the imminence of catastrophe.

Pride could no longer sustain him at the end; not even pain

could project itself as a challenge. Just paranoid fantasies of federal agents swooping out of the Idaho mountains to seize what remained of his privacy, his money, the struggles and secrets that he had banked craftily in his mind. The life was frozen now. Africa, Spain, Paris in the twenties—all were to disappear into what his son called "Fort Hemingway." Celebrated throughout the world, he had retreated into the harshest isolation of his life. Fort Hemingway stands over its owner, the immense symbol of his life's end, a blockhouse gravestone for the manhood he had demonstrated to all of us.

> It had been purchased early in his illness, but seemed to presage it. Set well back from the road, it was an almost bunkerlike blockhouse, built of poured concrete to last two hundred years, an ideal buttress against the world, and as safe a refuge as could be found for a paranoid. It lacked only catwalks and an electrified fence to be as secure as Trotsky's redoubt in Mexico.[9]

I wish that Hemingway had paused before he pulled the trigger of the most famous shotgun in American literary history. I wish he had tried to frame a sentence in which he told us what he had learned of the failure of heroism, the inadequacy of courage, the ceaseless trials of measuring up. I feel that he still owes us that debt, a single sentence into which he might have put all that he knew about the ambiguities of manhood. This man we created out of his own image was stripped naked at the end, an imprisoned spirit no longer even directing himself.

In this world, each of us is consumed by those energies set loose by his own failures. How terribly we want something more for our fathers and teachers. And we deserve that. Or at least I would like to think so.

FOOTNOTES

1. It is important to remember the extent to which Hemingway set himself up as a "man's writer," in much the same way as, for example, a poet such as Adrienne Rich today sees herself as embodying a woman's point of view in her work. Attempts to rescue his reputation today sometimes even take the form of trying to make him a contemporary who anticipated our own sexual attitudes. An essay by Aaron Latham in the October 16, 1977 issue of *The New York Times Magazine* argues, rather unconvincingly I think, for Hemingway's androgyny and sexual passivity. Such excursions into literary psychology, however, do little more than inform us of why psychology and literary criticism are still such awkward bedfellows.

2. *"Consciousness of death,"* writes Ernest Becker, "is the primary repression, not sexuality." See *The Denial of Death*, p. 96.

3. For details of the life, I have relied on *Ernest Hemingway: A Life Story* by Carlos Baker (New York, 1969). But I have also read all the other memoirs and biographical sketches of the man.

4. Norman Mailer, "Henry Miller: Genius and Lust, Narcissism," *American Review 24,* ed. Theodore Solotaroff (April, 1976), p. 5.

5. Anthony Alvarez, *The Savage God: A Study of Suicide* (New York, 1973), p. 84.

6. Hemingway's inability to create women characters is probably his greatest limitation as a novelist. And it can, I suspect, be attributed to his need not to see women as anything other than emblems of manhood. With a few notable exceptions, the women in his fiction are boring and two-dimensional. Most of them seem to fold into the backgrounds in which men play out their destinies.

7. Becker, p. 246.

8. See Donald Honig's *Baseball When the Grass Was Green*.

9. Gregory H. Hemingway, *Papa: A Personal Memoir* (Boston, 1976), p. 116. "That my father would tell me the truth about his mental illness was unthinkable," writes Hemingway's doctor son. "Something physical, sure. But mental, never. He was too much my father, my model, a whole generation's model, and he thought he'd fail those whom he had wanted so desperately to teach, had tried all his life to teach. He'd let us down if he went crazy. They said it was his machismo. I think it deserves a nobler word. His act of deception was as much one of love as it was of pride."

Chapter Five
Bodies and Minds

These slow men from the Iron Range—
how they laugh
watching their clean sons skate.
    —Roland Flint, "High School Hockey in Minnesota"

I

IF IT IS PAIN WHICH FORCES THE BODY to verify its own existence, it is the body itself which insists that men can come to terms with what they are, that they can live in the world actively, as men. This is a fact that men resist, particularly in America, where the body/mind controversy continues to rage. A man is either a mental or a physical being, and most men would be content were pain to stifle all protest from their bodies. So much of a man's life is spent in efforts to placate the body's insistent demands, to relieve himself of the mind's anxieties and to protect and nurture the physical. Fifty-year-old disco princes intent on "letting it all hang out" or Central Park joggers beating against the unhealthy, filth-ridden air remind us of man's urgent desire for regeneration. The body consciousness we see all around us is not, I believe, merely the latest American manifestation of our love affair with youth. No, for such self-conscious agonies are closer to the rejection of youth. Rather, the very act of letting the body take command is the key to a simple redemption.

I find myself wondering whether speculation about the body reduces the genuine pleasure it offers. I know that as I drive along the West Side Highway on my own pilgrimage to my particular shrine of the physical, I feel trapped by the very rush of anticipation I experience. Momentarily, I try to ignore the anticipation as I maneuver the car around this

115

Monday's potholes. I am going to work out in the gym in New Jersey. I avoid the potholes by straddling lanes, inured by now to the irritated horns of other drivers. I am looking forward to working out, the one activity which rids me of my excess of consciousness and mannered maneuvering. I push aside the phrases still spinning through my head and focus on the job awaiting me.

I think about strapping myself to the machines, I think about lifting weights until I manage to suspend oblivion into a distant future, so that all I am able to feel is motion, not even weights working against muscles or the effort I am putting into it or even the quality of my performance. The motion itself is reduced to something banal, enviable; motion slipping repetitively into motion until there is nothing else. I think about the feeling and I laugh with expectant happiness. Games for boys. Adolescent posturings elevated into a psychology of being—more than was ever intended from games. Is it any wonder that sportswriting is so plebian a trade?

My workouts are anchored to the solidity of habit. On days I go to the gym, I eat a large breakfast and I think about not eating lunch and that, too, is part of the expectation. On those days, I want nothing but the flow of movement. At such times, I am picked up, seized by the desire to bang my body against everything that stopped me in my own past from realizing important moments. After thirty-one years of walking on the crutches, my elbows are arthritic and my fingers have begun to numb from the creeping paralysis of nerves damaged by too much punishment, too many lifts on the crutches, too many banisters and floors and concrete walks. I have always insisted on the capacity of *my* arms to create the existence I want. But in the gym I push aside all such obstacles. In the gym I reinforce the necessity of motion, the silence of my body reduced to dimensions that break off from time. In the gym, there are no endings, just a series of beginnings strung together. A man's need. My need.

I pull into a parking space in front of the liquor store, lock my car, and walk the thirty or so feet to the gym, my anticipation growing with each step I take. Motion and manhood: a simple equation. I open the door and note once again that the gym is well-carpeted, a deep red and blue plush into which my crutches sink ever so slightly. It is all modern and chrome and the heavy black vinyl covering of the Nautilus machines indicates the exertion it inspires. The machines are simply there, passive but immediate, designed to placate all the bodies on whose sweat they make their demands.

The locker room is filled with New Jersey high school athletes who are here to force their bodies past artificial peaks. The horseplay quiets as I enter, the boys retreat into a more reserved hum of readiness. I can hear the instructor talking about breathing and motion outside the locker room. I remove tie and shirt, keys and wallet, pull the gray sweatshirt out of my workout bag, lock up, and walk back to the machines. The high school boys stand aside and several elbow each other as I pass. Being older invests me with authority. I enjoy it. I strap myself into the pullover machine after the seat has been adjusted for my height by Jim, the instructor. I cradle my elbows in the padded armrests, grasp the chrome bar, close my eyes to block out the world, and brace myself for the first pull of the afternoon.

I work the pullover incessantly, driving against it, trying to press my mind and body into the motion. Expelling air from my lungs with each pull. Fifty-pound weight on the pulleys. I have decided to lift for twelve minutes, which means that I will have to do three hundred lifts without stopping, until sweat blends into motion. As I near the two hundredth pull, I can feel my body reduced to its own coordinates, as if I had mastered my geometry of motion. The trick is to do it with arms alone. Not to try to compress the cripple's years into fantasy. Here there is nothing to stand in my way. As I pull forward and fight the weight going back, I do not dream of anything at all; I am interested only in the motion which completes me. I consciously try to work the muscles slowly, correctly. Pace one-two-three-four-five—one; one-two-three-four-five—two. My mind blanks out. The rest of the gym is visible but distant from my needs.

I ride the motion like a spirit that has slipped into the bloodstream and is now coursing through my body, a roller-coaster of repetition. The counting at one hundred sixty-eight and the sweat flowing freely now and my body tied into the rhythm and nothing else at all. I feel alone, invulnerable, each motion a separate validation of my existence. I concentrate on breathing correctly. As I pull down, I push the air out; as I fight the weight on the way back, I breathe in. Lifting is simple, technique transformed into motion, until the point arrives when the motion is all and the harsh grueling repetitions emerge as their own vindication. No explanations are necessary. Just do it. The rest of the world can be easily blotted out, denied.

All the purpose of the exercise—to keep in shape, to build muscles so strong that compensation on crutches will be even more simple, to hammer out the rhythms that will enable me to survive within my own skull as well as in the world outside—seems distant now. What I love so about lifting is the lack of complexity. Motion simplifies life down to questions of technique, energy, and strength. It demands concentration, yet it absolves me from thinking. The kind of determination it calls for lacks elegance; its movements contain no inherent beauty.

The gift it offers is the assertion of the body's need to exist on its own terms. A man's primacy. All around me, the world conspires to deny a man's needs. But not here. I do not have to think about profession, wife, children, students, responsibilities; I do not have to consider my role as a teacher, the reviews of my last book, whether or not to buy a new car, family feeling, the inner exile of Soviet intellectuals or whether the Nazis should be permitted to march in Skokie.

Only the. kindness of motion. No abstractions to plague the clear lines of physical being. I pump away, filled with a surging joy. By now, all voices around me have been blocked out. In lifting, I get beyond the rest of my senses. Motion alone tells me how good I am.

II

BODIES HAVE CREATED THE CONDITIONS of their own exertions. Running, jumping, even standing still, American manhood seeks to get beyond the limitations of our time. If there is nothing left to struggle with in the landscape, we create games for men. And a vocabulary to match. There are moments when the military metaphors which dominate our conversation about sport catch those reminders of the body's purpose. Thick-muscled bull-shouldered football players, lean distance runners blending their small bodies into the wind, potbellied pitchers gazing squint-eyed into the catcher's dumpy form: all these dull forms of combat which dictate to what William James called "the moral equivalent of war."

Is it this that clutters the minds of sportswriters who spend their days endowing the remnants of childhood play with a serious value system? Their language strains with their task: to examine how these games form our myths, emblazon our past, create a dependable vacuum of intellect in which all limitation can be exceeded. They can be trusted because they were trusted when we were boys. Time freezes. The words address themselves to the sharp nostalgia of men who are determined to recapture that which time has cheated them of. Why do I sometimes feel as if I would trade the man who has endured for the subtle tremor of ten-year-old wrists again gripping a bat which has just made clean contact with a ball? Why do so many of the men I talk to—doctors, lawyers, teachers, superintendents, waiters—respond so personally to the records and rituals of time past? Why do I feel immediate sympathy for the aging pitcher on television who has given up a career as a television broadcaster to stumble once again through the minor leagues in search of a moment or two that will negate all past failures?

I discover the answer in the gym. It is not the adolescent's recordkeeping, the need to quantify performance or balance my own emotional bookkeeping. Alone with the motion, the mind blanks out into these gratifying hard-won rhythms, and the joy I feel turns out to be as much as the fantasies of childhood promised. For me. For any man. There is a vital need for the body to perform within one's preset boundaries and limitations. This performance is not something a man can make light of, not, at least, when he knows he is working within the rules of the game. The realities of technical competence and disciplined effort simply exist on their own.

Mind, body, time and performance—all must be obliterated. Working out in the gym fills me with a sweet emptiness; it is one of the things I need to maintain a sane perspective on life. The most inessential of movements proves necessary. All during the workout, I am aware of how silly I will feel if I think about what it is I am actually doing. As an intellectual, after all, I can only be expected to keep my "soul and reason in good trim," as Montaigne says. A willing prisoner, I want only to be trapped in motion.

As a boy, you learn which tests are proper, which measurements can be verified. You learn that there is a proper way to challenge yourself.

"Young dogs and small boys fight 'for fun,' with rules limiting the degree of violence; nevertheless the limits of licit violence do not necessarily stop at the spilling of blood or even at killing."[1] The attraction of matching the individual to those skills he wants to control proves to be powerful for each of us.

It is not by accident that sport isolates men more than other activities. And this is as true of team sports as it is of lifting weights or running through Central Park. All of the rhetoric about communion with the self or communion with nature misses the point of what such activity does: It feeds a man's need to structure his fantasies. Most runners I speak to confess that they are usually oblivious to their surroundings. "It's the motion and the rhythm," my marathon-runner friend tells me. "That's what you do it for. I'm much more aware of the pain than of where I am. Because the pain is what you have to live with, but you know if it gets too bad then it breaks the motion. So the threat of it is there even when the pain itself is absent."

And with just that awareness I move through the gym, strapping my body to the exertions of one machine after the other. Chest pulls, bicep pulls, shoulder presses—I work each movement to its proper angle, as if I were driving the Indianapolis 500 and my very life depended upon my concentration. No matter how familiar the patterns, I must clearly remember what I have done before. Feelings about pain are projected onto the machine. Witness to my performance, uncaring, lacking a voice, the machine is both friend and enemy. Nothing else so clearly testifies to the control I exert. Rhythm dominates, motion repeats itself. I search for the moment when effort becomes automatic; I advance upon my own body's possibilities, and force it out of its own security. Motion guarantees the uniqueness of my manhood. The pain in my shoulders is a ripe soreness. The quick play of self against circumstance is what I have learned to enjoy about the cripple's difference from the normal. But I am thinking too much now. I want to do nothing more than lift. For the self and the silence both.

III

IT HAS BECOME FASHIONABLE of late to point out that sport
has had a more powerful impact upon our conception of
manhood than we have been able to admit until recently. Like
so many claims in America, it is offered as revelation. Sports
consciousness, we are told, is the single most fundamental
awareness of the American mind. Professors and jocks rival
each other in the attempt to teach us our lesson. The very
nation itself is reduced to a reflection of our passionate involvement with sport.

> For us, sport has entered the fabric and structure of our
> whole way of life. Sport is a constant, a model, a value
> system. It is our strength and our weakness, our re-
> deemer and destroyer (though Shelley would shudder at
> this application of his words). Intellectually and philo-
> sophically, emotionally and psychologically, sexually
> and physically, sport governs our lives. . . . We must go
> further and recognize that our system as a whole has
> become, that the U.S.A. *is,* a jockocracy.[2]

The passage speaks to that relentless American need to pin
a label on what is seen. Sport provides form and definition to
those aspects of a technocratic society which demand skill,
dedication, and discipline—and demand them not only of the
professional athlete but of the advertising executive who runs
or the janitor who plays softball once a week to break the
siege of his own body. The "jockocracy" is too obvious a
target, particularly in a nation in which men believe that they
can deal with their problems by combining them into a single
entity. The athlete may be a contemporary hero, but he is not

necessarily a model of manhood—or, for that matter, of anything else.

Sport takes one beyond the self by narrowing the outside
environment, as does any activity which demands specific
skills and which can only be acquired with discipline. Behind
the adulation of athletes in America is a belief in the value of
skills which have been tested. There are obvious dangers to
this, chief among them being the widening of the split between body and feeling. And this, of course, goes far beyond
game-playing. In America today we have what has come to be
called "sportfucking," where the body is expected to perform
at sex while it remains totally divorced from the idea that
there is another person involved. Such sexual recordkeeping
is probably related to the statistics which measure the batting
average in baseball or a quarterback's success in passing. The
idea of *having* all available women is cleanly cut off from the
actual body one couples with. Even in a good deal of recent
American fiction, sexual activity is described as a form of
combat, and takes up the comparative imagery once reserved
for competitive games. So many literary characters—both
men and women—are simply sexual timekeepers.

It is curious to see how sport helps shape our ideas—not
just of sexuality, but also of manhood. Participation in
sport—and this, I suspect, is true even for the beer-guzzling
overweight crowds that roar their approval of Ohio State's
football team on autumn weekends—affirms values that are
both more immediately productive and simpler than those
from other areas of American life. Sport is not a training
ground for success in life, nor is it the sole determinant of the
responsibilities of manhood. Still, sport *is* absorbed into our
need for autonomy, for an existence in which skill conditioned by discipline creates a sense of adventure for both
participant and observer. It may very well be that America's
fascination with sports activity is what actually saves us from
becoming a "jockocracy." The body's demand for excellence
is perhaps one of the few remaining areas of an autonomous

existence. It certainly fulfills a need for the kind of potency which is absent in so much else in our world.

Perhaps our problem in coming to terms with sports is their meretricious commercialization. A sports vocabulary has been plastered over games for boys. The intention is to make that activity more accessible; the reality is an enormous strain placed upon our sympathies. Writing about sport in America—and this is, on the whole, as true of sports fiction of some quality as it is of the daily sports pages—has been remarkably mediocre, mythicizing what should be clear and simple and forcing upon it an inappropriate complexity. Why the need to justify that expenditure of energy, that particular effort that defines endurance and skill? A ballet dancer works with a more complex and dedicated integrity than a basketball player (and usually for a lesser reward), but how many in this nation of men envy the ballet dancer? Men are still in love with what they believe sport can verify. "I'm becoming a jock in my old age," my Viennese-born physicist friend laughs. "It's not so simple an instrument, this body." What, I ask, does he want from it? "Not from it," he insists. "For it. For the first time in my life, my body seems real to me. You know, I came to this country at the age of thirteen. And I could never understand the American fascination with sport. The thing is total. Even the people who hate it . . . they hate it totally. It haunts them. Only the way I feel now when I play raquetball or I run . . . as if my body is the one thing I know that doesn't threaten to become an abstraction. It's the one thing I feel I can depend on."

He does not call it manhood; after all a man is not just the sum of his physical effort. He is something more, something greater. But neither is he a disembodied mind. And he is not a mere reflection of what other men have done before him. Even the statistics and rituals with which men seek to define performance are ultimately invested with a personal meaning. The contradictions are apparent in each of us. We want what the man within feels he lacks. For my friend, it is the body as its own fluid totality; for me, as I work out in the gym, it is the merger of my mind and body to a single strand of silence and will. Mind avails, presses against the body's dilemmas, insists on *its* existence, *its* primacy. I am thrown into my own trophy-hunting as I try to pull my mind back from its sweated rest. Each of us bangs at the gates, intent on passing through his own myths, fears, that collection of savage seductions with which he must try his man.

IV

HE IS AN OLDER STUDENT. Perhaps in his late forties, even fifty. A big man, at least three inches taller than six feet, slightly round-shouldered. But he still walks with a certain ease, his body resisting the demand of middle age that he surrender. He approaches the desk after the class has ended on the first day of the new semester. He smiles, says shyly, "Excuse me, professor"—a European tone with a New York accent, the word "professor" investing me with some subtle magic. For a moment, I wonder whether he is here by mistake. I search his face and before I know it I create a history for him. I decide that he is retired. A belt manufacturer who made his money and then, at the age of forty-eight or nine, madness staring him in the face, decided that he would now, here, still in this world of American men, squeeze dreams of sanity from the rock he carries within his heart—all those books read in secret, the longing for something better, finer, less oppressive. I am wrong. But not altogether.

"What you said at the beginning of the class. . . ." I look at him quizzically. "About baseball. You said baseball defies anarchy." I nod. "I used to play." Then I remember the name on the registrar's card. And I remember watching him work once at the Stadium. He was what we used to call "a good journeyman pitcher," before the inflated salaries and pampered egos threatened to make such a creature obsolete. Big body, big Jewish nose, good curve ball. Not overpowering. A good journeyman pitcher made the most of the skills he possessed. Nothing to excess. He could hit well for a pitcher, too.

It was a simpler time. But now, even the simplicity of baseball—that terrible boy's passion that I will carry with me to the grave—has been mangled by the superstar vocabulary and the jock itch for recognition that seizes sportswriters and college professors alike as they tell us how to live within those fantasies *they* deem legitimate. But in a simpler time, I remember watching him pitch—a clear definition of role.

"I never thought of it as defying anarchy, professor," he laughs. "When you're doing it, you don't think about what it means." He pauses, removes a pack of cigarettes from his open-necked sportshirt. "Is it all right if I smoke?" I nod. "I knocked around with a few clubs. Detroit, Chicago. Wound up in the National League." He blows smoke at the blackboard. "I'm going to think about what you said." He leaves.

In the weeks that follow, I learn that he is in class because he now wants to become a teacher, to see whether he can spend a few years in the ghetto schools working with blacks and Puerto Ricans. He wants to be "a *whole* man"—and that phrase is his own, part of his stubborn insistence on the needs he now feels. I discover that I like him, even admire him for his naïve desire to transform blacks and Puerto Ricans in the swamps of the Bronx and Brooklyn through the magic names, as he himself feels transformed. Only this time it will be Emerson and Melville and Twain, names that he will bring out of their strangeness into the world, instead of DiMaggio and Mays and Clemente. Perceptions of the past, responses to each graded situation. He has an immense appetite for it all, wanting to find what the books have promised to show him after all these years. He is willing to push his anxieties to the side as he shunts away what held him back in the past.

One day, as I am out for a walk, I meet him in the street and we drop into a neighborhood luncheonette to talk. He tells me how excited he is about reading Twain, that he is not quite certain he will be as excited by James. He does not trust Thoreau because he does not believe that a man can live as Thoreau expected him to live. I tell him I do not trust Thoreau either. What he really wants to talk about, it turns out, is why he entered college when he was closing in on fifty.

"I read about these salaries they pay big leaguers today. It doesn't hit me. I can't even feel sympathy for my own. I guess the ballplayers deserve it. It's a lousy life. I played big league ball for nine years. Before that, another eight in the minors. I knocked around for five years as an outfielder before I started pitching. It's funny. You try and figure out someone else's life and you discover it's your own. That's what I like with Twain. You get this feeling he never expects more from you than he would from himself. No one's really going to come out ahead anyway."

He sips his coffee. "This thing of mine with education . . . you don't mind if I talk to you about it." I shake my head. "I wanted to play ball ever since I could remember. Only that's just the beginning. I figured you had to be one thing or the other. You know, you work with your hands or you work with your head." I slip back into my own needs and see my body falling free of the braces and crutches, sliding off into its own past. At ten, I can hit a baseball farther than anyone I know. At forty, I want to do it again. "Playing ball reinforces it," he continues. "I thought at first it was a Jewish thing. It's not . . . it's American. A jock is a jock. Which means that he has no head, he's a clown right out of the funny pages. I didn't read newspapers, books, nothing, except for the *The Sporting News*. I read the sports pages in whatever town I was playing in. I would look for my name in the paper, like the other ballplayers. Reading damages the eyes, that's what we'd tell ourselves." He snorts. "You look at a book and you figure you'll go blind, you won't be able to find the strike zone." But in the books we find ourselves. In the books we run and cut loose from our moorings. He waves at the ceiling, disgustedly,

dismissing his past attitude. "We would make fun of ourselves. Each of us thinking he's half a man. Jesus, every man
I knew wanted someone to tell him he was as real as the next
guy. He could think, too. I had a good life. I'm not complain-
ing. Even moving through those minor league towns, you see
things. Twain would've liked that, travelling in the minors.
You see a lot."

He stretches his hands out on the table. They are big hands,
huge, bigger even than my own. I am very vain about my own
hands and I find myself thinking that a man's hands shape
his conception of what he is. I would like to have a pitcher's
hands. "Some men grow up and they cut themselves in half.
A man is a body. Two hands, two arms, two legs, a face with a
nose and two eyes, a back, two feet, a cock. Everything guaranteed to make you the genuine article. Yeah, I wish Twain
could've written about us. After I was washed up, it still
didn't get to me. You only have a few years. An arm gets sore.
Or you just lose your stuff. Anything. I saved a few bucks. I'm
finished as a pitcher, I earn even more money as a liquor
salesman. Money is money. Only I begin to wonder who I am.
I'm forty-three, I'm getting these terrible migraines, and then
I'm on the couch. I wanted the couch so much that the first
time I'm on it I'm crying. I discover what I've always suspected—that I think I'm some kind of horse's ass. I'm surplus
material. Nothing. And at forty-three I'll never see my curve
ball again and I'm tired of selling liquor and I'm tired of
pretending I'm some hotshot kid with women. I want to settle
down, read, think. Damn it, you're not a man if you can't do
what a man is supposed to do. You're not a man if all you do
is throw a ball. Can you imagine? Afraid to read because I
don't want to strain my eyes. I'm protecting my career. ' He
pauses, stares down at the table. "And I believe it. I'm afraid
not to. All ballplayers believe they're not real. At least the
ones I remember did. Oh, we're probably good enough physically. Half the guys I knew in the majors would walk
through concrete on a bet. But deep down, each of us is

convinced he's dumb. It's a kid's game." It takes great effort
for him to say this. I think again of what I wanted as a child,
what I still want. His hand shakes as he lights another cigarette. "This world is a son of a bitch. Doesn't leave a man a
way out. Either you're one thing or the other. And you always
figure it's going to be better if you can become that other
thing. Only you discover that it isn't better. It's just not
worse."

"What kind of a man do you think you are now?" I ask.

"Better than I was. I don't mean it's better to read books
than to throw strikes. Only I don't want my life formed by a
talent that's no more than an accident. I'm not ashamed of
having been a ballplayer. But I want more." He draws a circle
with his right forefinger in the wetness left by the coffee cup
on the formica table. "It's tough to have to fight just to be
what every man should have the right to be. Jesus, to have a
mind. That's it."

"How did it change?" I ask.

"Listen. The first time I read a book from cover to cover, I
was forty-four years old." He shakes his head from side to
side. "Forty-four. You know what that is, to be forty-four and
read a book?"

V

THE BODY-MIND WAR RAGES against American men, against
each man's image of his potential. The dichotomy splits men
apart and it forces them to categorize each other. No one
wants to be a perpetual child, doomed to live within the static
confines of children's games. And no one wants to be so
imprisoned by the demands of his mind that he extends the
very myths he wishes to escape. Men cannot live with their
bodies and they cannot live beyond them. Body consciousness
locks into manhood, denying the credibility it was intended to
affirm. A man's body, after all, is an individual self.

I watch my fifteen-year-old son and his friends drive against the schoolyard basket, jump, fingerarch their shots just like the professionals they have studiously observed at Madison Square Garden. What is it, I wonder, that they feel compelled to demonstrate to each other? A competence that enacts the roles all men share and must deal with? The body silent but insistent in its demands. The body never sufficient to give a man the kind of control he seeks but still defining him as a man. Not an easy gift to live with. Short, tall, thin, fat—a parade of body types which, however secretly, help codify the existence of men. Why can't these adolescent boys reach beyond their limitations, arching shot and substance against that imaginary seven footer standing his ground? No different from my own attempts to hammer my body into motion, to rid myself of its demands by creating those innumerable tests of machine and weight. The body itself needs to create the man, and its need forces each of us into dependable patterns: five more shots, ten more lifts. Small deaths for clear rituals. For men discover that neither mind nor body is sacrosanct. They exist in a curious relationship; each condemns a man to himself.

The pattern is apparent everywhere. Just as the ex-ballplayer searches for the right to call his mind his own, so do the intellectuals I know now play with their fantasies of physical prowess. The body's betrayals are always personal. Like folds of flesh within a fat man, the body reveals its everchanging formations. The body's accomplishments are more transitory, more accidental than the mind's. And yet, so much more ego is invested here. Mind lives beyond itself, but body never does. An athlete who can no longer perform violates our memories of our own unspent youth. Who can wipe memory clean of the aging Willie Mays on his return to New York from San Franscisco? His failures were shards cast deep into *our* memories, forcing us to question what the grace and strength of the body could be, had been, when manhood simply existed and talent was enough for him and for us.

VI

I SIT IN A HOLIDAY INN in Shawnee, the cool dimness
nursing my eyes against relentless hours of driving through
Arkansas and Oklahoma. In the adjacent booth, five high
school basketball coaches talk and laugh. Laughing at the
bodies. Slamming their ownership of the bodies against the
table with loud voices. All-Star games between Texas and
Oklahoma in the mid-June heat. "You see that nigger boy?"
Laughter growing round the table. "Stick a poker up that
boy's ass," says another, "he don't jump no higher." More
laughter. Bidding on bodies as though they were meat on the
rack.

But is it any different from the ways adolescent boys learn
to measure themselves all through the country? Run farther,
piss longer, shoot better, hit harder. "Ahhh," my son whispers to me one evening, the exaggerated hoarseness of his
voice sliding his triumph out like a silver dollar rolled onto
the kitchen table, "you should have seen me on the court
today. I faced the nation! Ahhh, the *naashun*." And he
laughs, too, because he knows that no further explanations
are necessary. It is his body, his expectations, which he
claims to defend. But he is as much the victim of his expectations as the black who jumps in Shawnee, Oklahoma, and the
coaches who skim their talent for living and laughter.

The mind/body dichotomy anchors itself in all men. It
lives in the not-so-secret pain of young black men in the
schools, who emerge as creatures of the nightmares they have
been bequeathed, mindless bodies probing toward long-mus-
cled grace—and never mind the wizened and the fat and the
drugged who cannot get off their asses. Myths will be served!
It lives in the envious longing of young whites watching the
black bodies and wondering why the smooth grace is not

theirs, too, wondering whether it was something their ancestors possessed before their minds were crowned. No matter
that in the sixties, body and mind, black and white, were
married: Neither believes in that union any longer. The play-
grounds of America are transformed into ethnic battlefields.
The air is thick with old grudges and new liberations, each
played off against the other. The myths of groups cleave to
their playground styles. No man ever learned tolerance playing the games of children—not in New York, and not in
Shawnee, Oklahoma.

In my car, I sit and watch the game in the schoolyard,
unobserved. Body twists against body. Even from where I am
sitting, at least thirty feet away, the savage contempt on the
faces is clearly visible. On one side, two whites; on the other,
a black and a light-skinned Hispanic. Which hegemony will
lay the claim? In the beginning, the contest seems even. They
move against each other's skills. The black is graceful, fluid,
but he has bad hands. He keeps losing the ball out of bounds
when the light-skinned Hispanic whips it to him. The whites
are stronger, more bullish. They concentrate on the ball, and
they help each other out. I watch as one of the whites drives
the baseline past the basket, turns in mid-air, then drops a
short pass off to the other white under the basket who blows
the shot, bulls past the light-skinned Hispanic, seizes the
rebound and stuffs it home.

As they play, the four grow angrier. I imagine them playing
out fantasies of death, as they drive deadened aspirations
around the court. Neither skill nor talent will dominate, but
rather each body's need to differentiate itself from the others.
Tempers flare as white and Hispanic collide in mid-air, each
finger-snapping at the ball as it bounces out of bounds. Words
crash against other city noises, expletives intended to protect
not talent but a sense of honor. Trading style for manhood,
they shove each other. The white is eager for the confrontation. He is bigger, stronger, the Hispanic touched the ball last,

he insists. The Hispanic holds his ground. The black stands, hands on hips, shakes his head and wipes his face with his sleeve. The other white separates the Hispanic and his friend. "Choose!" the black demands. "Damn it, choose!" They choose, the white wins, his sense of justice reinforced. The Hispanic shrugs. He has held onto himself.

It is easy enough to dismiss this awkward display of nerve, muscle, bone, fiber and cartilege stripped to a command performance. But self-respect is probably the last possession left either of them. As I watch the game resume, I am filled with a terrible sense of their pain. What will the Hispanic salvage from this encounter? If he were bright enough to reason through it, he might yet be all right. But I can see that he lacks poise, his temper will destroy him by the time he is twenty-one. And the white boy, too, struggling against a world that discounts his body. *Don't screw around with me!* That thing one grew up with refuses to change—it used to grate on me. And now I sit in the car, feeling that I must make my peace with it. I watch body go against body, hands against hands. Man against man, everything squared away in the fight to prove endurance. There is something inevitable about it—and something sickening, too.

Mind and body war against each other, twist, turn, struggle, each trying to break to the surface and declare its primacy. This is each man's war. Some throw themselves into the world of body and make a triumph of their fear; others wait, ensconced in the suburbs of their minds, IBM and Einstein and god himself all original patents, mind exploding energy, seizing stars, universes, galaxies, minds distancing themselves from all bodies—black, yellow, red, white, brown—as they hurtle through their self-created firmaments. All sex in the head, all money in the bank. And men remain divided creatures, protecting themselves from the moment when mind and body clasp hands and kiss, a shy surrender for each.

FOOTNOTES

1. Johan Huizinga, *Homo Ludens: A Study of the Play Element in Culture* (Boston, 1955), p. 89.

2. Neil D. Isaacs, *Jock Culture, U.S.A.* (New York, 1978), p. 17

Chapter Six
Frames

I Licked the Big C Once Before and I Can Do It Again!
—Tabloid headline quoting John Wayne
on his struggle with cancer

I

IN THE MOVIES, WE MET NOT OURSELVES but visions of what we might yet become—American men. My own stolen moments of never-forgotten frames separate the man I am today from the man I first envisioned when the frames captured me. In memory, I slide down into the red plush seats of the Mosholu Theater on Bainbridge Avenue, oblivious even to the candied smell of the darkness and the two friends flanking me. We have come here together, sweat-grubbed hands clutching thin dimes, from the Saturday morning baseball game. It is a ritual we share with boys all through the country, as we exchange one set of heroes for another.

But the landscape I actually see as I drive through America presses against the heart's affections. This Texas Panhandle belongs to those frames from the Hollywood dreams, and I cannot shake my old impressions even as I struggle against its monotonous rhythms. The sky is blue and ceaseless, the way it was in the movies—an immensity of sky against which a single man on a horse invariably moved. I can still see that lone rider, the creation of some tarnished dream of manly independence. How clearly it was presented to me; how easily I made it mine. I whistle past the occasional early morning pick-up barreling west on Interstate 40 and I see a different landscape from the one before me; the one made of myth, of movies. And I still cannot give it up—not willingly. For it

restores manhood from the image to life, molded by the imagination's own Hollywood touch. I needed to dream as much as
anyone else. No truth like that of the screen. "Like my peers,
I discovered America in the movies of the thirties, those
gargantuan, crass contraptions whereby Jewish brains projected gentile stars upon a gentile nation and out of their own
immigrant joy gave a formless land dreams and even a kind
of conscience."[1] My manhood has been formed by the frames.

As I plow through this western space, I understand the
collective need to dream. This is a desolate land, but it addresses its very emptiness to a man's sense of being the best of
the best; both American and man, playing to an audience that
understands that the one confers distinction upon the other.
For the films I watched as a boy of ten provided me with
possibilities. I sat in my seat, wanting to be a man, impatient
with all that told me I was yet a child. I hungered to be a true
American, since, however much I might have loved the
warmth of that transplanted Eastern European community of
which I was still a peripheral part, I was smart enough to
understand what counted in this "American" world: The
movies counted, the fist counted, the courage of the single
man against the landscape counted, the ability to endure
punishment counted, and the ability to project oneself against
the future counted—perhaps more than anything else.

For future and past melded in the movies. You could sniff
the cool opportunities in the darkness. No deaths to die that
were not valiant, American, eminently natural. No dead ends
of apathy or indifference. Like a glove to the hand, the movies
fit. The frames spoke to us, advanced our coming of age,
enfolding it into the rituals which we shared with those men
who had come before us. They promised that we would be-
queath the idea of such a manhood to our sons, and they in
turn to their sons. The world had not yet sprung death loose,
not on me, not on my friends. Sheltered images spoke to us,
adolescents waiting in the wings.

II

THERE IS A QUALITY TO MOVIE CRITICISM and analysis that mocks the very art it seeks to penetrate. For movies remain the treatment of myths where the intimacy of image and reality coalesce. The movies which form us descend from a past which is both individual and collective, a past which denies the pretentiousness of the film industry, the innumerable studies of popular culture, and the rows of books about film which analyze image and frame and sequence. In movies, even in speaking about movies, we fortify each other's illusions; we discover that we are like the films we discuss, the product not of a single director but of a collective reaction to the moments captured by the frames. For if Hollywood fed the imaginations of men (and obviously women, who were, after all, the majority of the audience), the imaginations of men fed Hollywood too. Michael Wood is correct when he writes that "movies purvey myths that exist outside the movies, but that also feed on their movie career."[2]

Inevitably, the adult moviegoer remains blood brother to the child he was—for he takes the reality of what he sees on the screen at face value and seeks nothing beyond its image. Movies vindicate our memories, they assure us of the possession of our own pasts. Because the thing we see before us is so much larger than life, it is transformed by memory into a childlike innocence. We are reduced to our own aspirations for becoming—aspirations which have been given us by the movies; we search there not for truth but for verification. "The effectiveness of the western as a genre," writes the novelist Larry McMurtry, "has scarcely depended upon fidelity of detail, or, for that matter upon emotional validity."[3] We are given back exactly what we want to see. The

frames first catch us as children, and we learn, as a consequence, that we are not going to be able to make our images of
fantasy grow up along with us as we get older. The only way
in which we can maintain the simplicity of the gifts the
movies offer is to permit them to freeze us in time, even when
we are sufficiently aware to be able to approach them analytically. We become our own movies. And we slip into our
true selves, haunted by the "good guys" and "bad guys" of
our childhood, as we approach the screen once again.

I sit in the darkened classroom theater in New Mexico,
watching John Ford's *Stagecoach* along with the students in a
graduate seminar I am teaching. What interests me is that
particular personal fusion of space and time that *Stagecoach*
offers. Ford's ability to absorb the myth of the American West
on the screen is the recognizable quality of his genius. The
John Wayne who moves through the film as the Ringo Kid
magnifies all the realities about manhood we absorbed as
children. The fact that this film is a classic western is beside
the point. It goes beyond the necessity of analysis; it is my
past.

And not mine alone. Sitting beside me is an ex–Green Beret
who has come home from the chaos of Viet Nam ("I left the
bastards when they left me!" he tells me later over a drink) to
pursue a Ph.D. in history. A full-blooded Apache, he would
like to right the balance of history with simple solutions. He
has nothing but contempt for both sides in the underground
war that rages in New Mexico between Chicano and Anglo.
He sits in the darkened theater, away from the deceptive sun-
drenched calm of New Mexico, and he is hypnotized along
with the rest of us, by these images of American aspiration.
He is caught up in the film, even though he knows it is the
Apaches who will die. We sit alongside one another, two
skeptical American men, but Americans nonetheless—and
stare into the screen, accepting what is presented to us.

Stagecoach stands on its own. There is nothing beyond it,

nothing which exists outside of the screen's boundaries. One cannot conceive of the Ringo Kid existing anywhere but in this film. In *Stagecoach,* our manhood meets its American antecedents. Myths roll against each other. Even now, sitting alongside my Apache student and knowing that the Indians have been the wronged party, I go along with the film's point of view that the Indian is no more than a part of the landscape, to be swept aside by the power and determination of the American white man. Indians are part of the expectancy of combative manhood—even for my Apache student. For we have come to expect an outlaw manhood, one which exists, as it does in *Stagecoach,* beyond the stratifications of ordinary society, of decent people. For each of us sees the respectable characters as comic, whereas the outlaw, the Ringo Kid, is a personal legacy which has formed us.

A great deal of Deerslayer lingers in the still-young brow and laconic skills of John Wayne in *Stagecoach.* The character is stamped into his face—hard, clear, and simple—a product of the myth it will ultimately help to enforce. The Ringo Kid refuses to be circumscribed by home, environment, or law. In the society of the respectable men and women of Tonto, he is a pariah. In our eyes, however, he embodies what a man should be. Larger obligations take precedence over civilization. The Ringo Kid is going to kill the Plummers because they have murdered his father and brother. And the very passivity of Wayne's face on screen gives him and his mission an absolute manliness. Ford did not believe that men can create laws to live by as individuals; from what we know of him, he was far too conservative for that. But he understood that such concepts as responsibility, honor, and individual strength had dictated those cultural myths from which men created their manhood. Ringo is a lineal descendent of Natty Bumppo; he undertakes even vengeance through an obligation that goes beyond respectability. A man does not question his past; he simply adapts himself to the necessities of living within its embrace. The debt that Ringo must pay is not to his dead father and brother but to the idea of manhood which has been imposed upon him, which is imposed on most American men. What is fascinating about Ringo's view of his manhood is his essential lack of responsibility to society.

In the portrait of the Ringo Kid, manhood has been stripped of everything extraneous. It is, I suspect deliberately, a two-dimensional portrait. There is ultimately nothing really heroic about the Ringo Kid's actions; he simply assumes obligations because they are there. And yet, he is not self-serving, nor is he amoral. He is simply determined to do what must be done. He can love Dallas, the prostitute with the heart of gold, because she, too, is beyond respectability. But he also accepts her as an equal, recognizing that she is a more perceptive critic of respectable society than he. It is Dallas who describes the ladies of the Tonto Law and Order League, who have convinced their acquiescent husbands that she must leave town, as "worse than Apaches." And just as Ringo possesses the manly skills and virtues—courage, coolness under fire, a relationship to the environment that is both personal and distant—she possesses those womanly virtues which shall forever elude the young army wife who is so discomforted by the thought of sitting next to her. It is Dallas who helps the drunken doctor deliver the captain's lady's baby; interestingly enough, it is also Dallas who is really the film's portrait of motherhood, cradling the infant while its biological mother sleeps. The Ringo Kid combines energy with skill as Ford's representative man, but the burden placed on Dallas is even greater, for only women think and feel in the western myth. Men act—and in their actions prove themselves.

As seen in *Stagecoach*, the American man is outlaw; the American woman is the "good" prostitute. Each begins at a distance from respectable society and from each other, and each learns that the distance from society is necessary for survival but that the distance from each other can be over come. Ringo is the vital center of the film's action. The lives of the others are ultimately indebted to his manly skill, and to the simplicity with which he assumes those functions which, even if they exist outside of the law, are considered natural to the individual man. The other characters are all limited by their complexities: the doctor by the fatalism which leads him to drink his life away; the gambler by his cavalier southern romanticism; even the sheriff by his necessity of working within the law and order he has sworn to uphold.

Stagecoach was one of the last gasps of the idea of a specifically American manhood in film. Of course, the western that Ford refined so successfully in *Stagecoach* had many imitators, even *High Noon,* in which Gary Cooper plays a sheriff who simply seems a more sophisticated, aging Ringo Kid. Ultimately, however, the simplicity and directness in Ringo's approach to manhood proves an impossibility for him. The times catch up with the man. As Wayne portrayed him and as Ford conceived him, the Ringo Kid embodied both Hollywood's image of the assertion of American individualism and a nostalgia for the frontier man in a simpler time. But by the mid-1940s, the lone rider has already been replaced by the tough, cynical private eye, a "simple, harassed and nonintellectual character who is perpetually taking a terrific series of beatings . . . [and who] prefers to live alone, in spite of the fact that Southern California is . . . filled with seductive females; he is governed by an innate honesty, though he never quite knows himself what always prevents him from taking tainted money; and in his pursuit of justice he gets little help from anybody else, the police in particular being usually corrupt."[4] It is not by accident that the face of the young John Wayne is replaced in the consciousness of men by the craggier, more beaten-up faces of Humphrey Bogart and Robert Mitchum: Like the lone cowboy, the private eye works in a world in which he is his own moral center, deciding upon

what constitutes right and wrong, good and evil, discipline
and integrity. But the private eye, who still possesses the
singular virtues of the isolated American man, is himself soon
superceded, first by the G. I. in World War II films and then
by the worker and city streetcorner hero, best personified by
Marlon Brando in *On the Waterfront.*

It is worth noting that *On the Waterfront* is a film which
typifies the self-conscious virility of the cautious time in
which it was made. The fifties was a decade uncertain that it
possessed the very power of manhood this film insists upon.
The film purports to be both an emblem of manhood and an
emblem of America and it fails in each attempt. But although
it may be a meretricious film that stems from the worst of a
bad political and social climate, it is still a fascinating film for
the idea of manhood which it implicitly endorses.

The distance between the John Wayne of *Stagecoach* and
the Marlon Brando of *On the Waterfront* is far greater than
the distance between Deerslayer and the Ringo Kid. By the
1950s, Hollywood was consciously manipulating American
men. To the Hollywood mind, the enemies now confronting
the United States were far more dangerous than either the
forces of nature or the Apaches or even organized crime—and
far more devious, too. The Apaches in Hollywood myth are
cruel, hideously cruel (they stake their enemies out on the
desert to let them die of thirst and starvation), but they are
men, not just evil ideas incarnate. There is usually something
honorable about Indian manhood, too; after all, however un-
consciously, the audience in the theaters knew that *we* had
stolen the nation from *them.*

It is difficult to conceive of Terry Malloy, the young tough
of *On the Waterfront,* as a descendent of Deerslayer. For all
of his working-class simplicity, he is too defined a presence,
too involved with emotional depths and complexities. His
manhood reflects the tensions of a culture in which macho
has been elevated to a principle even though its failures are

overwhelmingly apparent. Like Ringo, he stands as the emblem of the manhood we are supposed to desire. But we are far less comfortable with Brando than with Wayne, far more aware, interestingly enough, of the extent to which our sympathies are being manipulated. Ringo is a creation out of the mythical past, the outlaw as heroic man, a last paean to the possibilities of man standing alone. Terry Malloy may lay claim to the same sense of outlawry, but there is no respectable world for him to work against. His entire world is *déclassé*. Those who ultimately inspire his rage and his Christlike resistance as he staggers to the loading dock to "go down there and get my rights" are themselves even further beyond respectability than he. Neither they nor he can serve as a true gauge of manhood in the film. In *On the Waterfront*, manhood is acted out against a political and social ambience which is itself hypocritical and self-righteous.

Karl Malden's priest is intended as the film's moral center, but he soon disintegrates into a figure left over from *Going My Way*. His own manhood comes down to talking like one of his waterfront congregation ("Gimme a beer!" he demands after a showdown with Terry) and he creates Christ in what, even for Hollywood, proves ludicrous—a kind of waterfront heavy with heart. In fact, this masculine but tender toughness is a consistent note in the film, intended in both Terry and the priest to portray an American type that is distinctive because it is American. Through the tenderness, everything soft is intended to be stripped away; but the artificiality is such that everything sentimental remains.

Brando is the manly center of this film, but he provides only a limited manhood—and this despite the fact that he is the finest film actor we have today. The simplicity of the Ringo Kid is subverted in this film into a series of virility poses, all of them designed to create an illusion of psychological sophistication, a more complex manhood and a richer, fuller sexuality. "The first fumbling gestures of androgyny, as an expression of alienation, began with Brando," writes Molly Haskell.[5] It would be impossible to write this of Wayne's Ringo Kid. *Because* of Wayne's two-dimensional act ing, the complexity that the modern man demands is kept at a distance. It simply doesn't count. The Ringo Kid is a mythical figure, in much the same manner as Achilles or the young David—he is an expression of the assumption of manhood. Perhaps that explains why Wayne's portrayal—so limited by the constrictions of American myth—is nonetheless ageless. For he never tried to portray a man of any depth; his job was simply to sustain the myths about manhood that make for easy recognition.

By the 1950s, men and women had both begun to lose confidence in the idea of a heroic masculinity. Freud descended like the Holy Ghost over Hollywood at the very point at which the power of the movie capital had begun to wane. The omnipotence of the manhood myths disintegrated; men discovered that they had to be explained, analyzed, their spontaneity curbed by their willingness to dissect themselves for others. In *On the Waterfront,* we see this in Brando's need to show Edie Doyle that he is more than "a bum," that he is, indeed, man enough to become her husband, to be integrated by her dead-faced convent charm into the rites of the clean and civilized. Ringo does what he must do; he cannot conceive of other choices, for throughout *Stagecoach* what is at stake is his obligation to his own worth as a man. Had Dallas not been on the stagecoach, Ringo would still have gone to Lordsburg to kill the Plummers. His life would not have been significantly different. But Terry Malloy becomes Edie Doyle's creature; he aims to please her. He comes a long way from when they first meet and, fist to the mouth, he offers the following idea of how a man lives: "Pfftt! Do it to him before he does it to you." By the end of the film, though, he is one more contemporary American man intent on uncovering his inner self, on claiming the psychological complexity of his

"I." In reality, however, Terry is neither tough nor tender. His yen for the security of middle-class need is in keeping with the film's politics and conception of manhood. Ringo's manhood as Wayne portrays it is rarely sexual, certainly not openly so. But Brando, following the patterns he had already established in both *A Streetcar Named Desire* and *The Wild One,* projects a specific sexual identity. Nonetheless, even his sexuality is directed at himself, another form of self-exploration. In both *The Wild One* and *On the Waterfront,* the women Brando yearns for are distant from him, removed from sexuality. For all of Terry Malloy's working-class grunting and for all of the subtle inwardness of Brando's acting, the character is another of life's losers. In the years that are to follow, one can see him, domesticated by Edie into the verisimilitudes of the middle class, perhaps once in a while sneaking off with the boys to the corner bar. His manhood, built upon the need to be tough, is finally directed at its own soft insides. He must maintain his distance from the man he once wanted to be. It is a peculiar paradox, perhaps worthy of the accommodations that the 1950s forced upon itself, that a man sensitive enough to love homing pigeons is not sensitive enough to love women—only to live up to them. The Ringo Kid was luckier. He did not have to examine the path along which his affections were carrying him.

III

I WATCH HIM MOVE ACROSS THE RESTAURANT, fists balled at his sides, body still powerful but thickened now, eyes puffy beyond the last drink or the memory of the one before that. He is heavier than he was in the movies, but I have no trouble recognizing him in this almost-deserted Roman trattoria. Outside, the rain sweeps in steady waves against the dark side-

walks. Deserted streets in a Roman winter. It is five o'clock
and there are no other customers in the restaurant. I am
sitting with my wife and our two-year-old son, who is propped
on two pillows in a straw-backed chair, his head just reaching
over the tabletop. He stares at the man who approaches our
table. The man halts furtively and watches Mark watching
him. I think of the frames, and I am suddenly sorry for him.
He shrugs, almost mimelike, and I wonder why I am always
so surprised at the simple gestures of men. Why do I remember them so vividly? The shrug of shoulders, the way a hand
grips a glass, the face approaching a break in the distance,
and now a body's drunken struggle for balance. His most
famous role, the one that was supposed to send him careening
through the Hollywood galaxy, was as a gangster. But he
doesn't look threatening now—just sad and tattered around
the edges and even a bit hesitant, as if he had to search for
the words with which to greet a two-year-old boy.

"Well," he says finally, staring at Mark. My wife looks
from his face to Mark's, smiles reassuringly. "Well, *you* look
like you still have it all." He does not slur but pauses between
the words, fingering the dark gray lapels of his suit. It is a suit
for a banker, not a gangster. Other than his speech pattern,
he does not seem as drunk as he is. Remnants of American
glory. The man who can hold his liquor is a real man—*that*
never made sense to me. It always seemed so callow a de-
struction.

His struggle for control makes me remember him the way
he was in the frames—an image, a presence created for the
needs of our perfection. I want him to make it, to *be* that
illusion once again, the figure I knew from the screen. In the
warm candle-lit Roman trattoria, our celluloid hero gropes
for language, gets momentarily beyond himself in his interest
in our son. "Have it all!" he repeats loudly. And as if he had
suddenly found the precise words he wanted, his face catches
a flicker of the strength I remember it had. "Have it all!

"And why not?" he asks, turning his attention to me. "Why the hell not? Christ, we're Americans, aren't we?" His laughter booms across the small restaurant, so that the bartender looks up from the pages of the sporting paper he has been studying. Then, seeing the actor, whom he obviously knows, he shrugs his shoulders and acknowledges the laughter, mine now, and Mark's, and the drunken Hollywood gangster's. We join in an American cacophony. I feel a bond with this man, for he is not, finally, a mere image—but a man, an American, struggling with the balance of what he is and of what he had once wanted to become. Only at such moments can one let go of the frames altogether. Holding fast and hanging on to what the man within wanted to be. No images, no frames. I would like to reach out and pull the poor bastard to me—for the furtive romance with which he touched my past and for this sense of laughing camaraderie we suddenly experience, we three men together.

IV

NO WONDER THAT THE ROLE of manly hero in the movies has progressively grown more confused: Men and women today eye each other like fighters searching for an opening. It simply makes sense that our tensions are reflected in the films we watch.

And there *is* something very appealing in the softness of the contemporary film hero. For once, *vulnerable* is fitting tribute—not the agonizing vulnerability we were brought up to make do with but a genuine concern for others caught by that yet-unformed web of circumstance and need that we call manhood. There is humor in such vulnerability, a gentle humor that points backward to the rich sexual comedies of Shakespeare, with their gender-switching disguises where one absurdity is piled upon the other. In such a world, one struggles merely to maintain a sexual balance.

The transition in the celluloid conception of the hero was some time in the making. In the films of the 1960s, men were on the verge of leaving the world of women altogether, of embracing each other's pain and accepting a cautious, adolescent male togetherness. We see this from the cowboy and Italian derelict in *Midnight Cowboy,* from the sexual scorecard keepers in *Carnal Knowledge,* from the pushers in *Easy Rider.* Above all, we see it in the outlaw pals of *Butch Cassidy and the Sundance Kid.* Here the Ringo Kid is sliced in half and divided between Paul Newman and Robert Redford, more fun-loving and playful, intent on nothing so much as having a good time. They eliminate the reality of women by making of Katharine Ross a kind of emotional ping-pong ball volleyed back and forth between them. In all of these films, the flight from women is defined in terms of male friendships that have all the intensity of Damon and Pythias and all the attractiveness, both sexual and emotional, that we once enjoyed in films about men and women. Newman and Redford have here turned around the traditional male/female struggle best exemplified in Spencer Tracy/Katherine Hepburn films. Their relationship anchors the film; even the violence has been deliberately stripped of all significance other than what it reflects of the bond between the two men. There is something distinctly asexual about the relationship between these two men, as there was between Tracy and Hepburn. It was always difficult to envision Tracy and Hepburn as sexual beings—and not because they were an unattractive couple (quite the contrary, they were perhaps the most attractive pair Hollywood ever created) but because they seemed to complement one another in every way, not just sexually. The opposition to one another in each of their movies arouses our interest, grows, irritates, finally culminates in a coming together of wit and articulateness. With Redford and Newman, there is a good deal of this, too; for all of their rugged individualism, theirs is a dreamy impractical relationship which disguises the masculine imperative for success with a conscious commitment to gaining each other's approval. Like Deerslayer and Chingachgook, Huck and Jim, they could join that archetypal American gallery of "asshole buddies." It is an attitude in film which has, admittedly, been seen before— witness *Gunga Din* in the 1930s. But in the sixties, it evolved as a far more conscious manipulation of male sympathies and male fears.

At present, however, the very idea of a Hollywood view of men and manhood has been turned around a full 180 degrees. In such films as *An Unmarried Woman* and *Coming Home,* the male hero emerges stripped of the hardness of past American conventions and willing to accept both his own newly sought emotional competence and the necessity that the woman he loves define her burgeoning selfhood. He has evolved into "the man to whom women turn as they try to change their lives; someone who is strong and affectionate, capable of intimacy, unthreatened by commitment, masculine without being dominating."[6]

The new male hero is willing to live with his own interior responses, consciously to tread the line between what society demands and what he sees himself as being. Compare, for example, Jon Voight's paraplegic Viet Nam veteran in *Coming Home* (1978) to Brando's paraplegic World War II veteran in Stanley Kramer's *The Men* (1950). In both films, there is great accuracy in dealing with the paraplegic's mannerisms. The rapport between body and wheelchair that both Brando and Voight achieve is enormously impressive. Their bodies seem to slide into the spaces they occupy, and the wheelchair becomes, for each of them, a kind of joyous freedom, something which they have captured for themselves and made their own.

But Brando's anger is a more powerful force than Voight's.

He is a tighter, more controlled actor, his fury rooted in the contrast between the football player he was and the paraplegic he becomes. The difference in the way each learns to exploit his situation is a significant comment on the shift in popular consciousness and the acceptance of new standards of manhood. Brando is very much a man of his time. He must prove that he is as good as the situation demands, that he remains within the American community, a man among men. In part, the tensions we see in him reflect the difficulties of emerging as *the cripple* in a society of normals; even more, however, they indicate that the American man is an adaptable creature, able to use the rough-and-ready masculinity to which he subscribes even before he is wounded.

Voight, on the other hand, assumes a cool supremacy over this American environment. He has nothing to prove, nothing to offer the world beyond the solid selfhood he has acquired. He has turned against American participation in the Viet Nam war: he even preaches an anti-war message to high school boys. There is a soft regality to Voight's portrayal of a paraplegic, which seems heightened by his beard and the quiescent muscularity of his body. Voight's character has paid his dues through his injury; he will now use it as the ultimately liberating force in his life. He will permit himself to rest with his manhood, free of the struggle other men must still go through. He is in the enviable position of having nothing left to prove, and so he can afford to be a soft king. In *The Men*, the paraplegics simply assume the competitive values of their society; in a sense, Brando's character, solidly muscular and clean-shaven, is still playing football in a wheelchair although the game is now for a livable life. The paraplegic in *Coming Home*, on the other hand, never even tries to regain his former self. Instead, he adjusts his manhood to new possibilities. We watch him rolling laughingly along the beach, suddenly aware of the beauty of the world; he takes joy in the mobility a car provides him. In his sexual encounters, it is he who becomes the normal's instructor. Sally's sexual awareness blooms under the paraplegic's tender erotic tutelage—she is suddenly free of the remembrance of her husband's mechanistic imprint on her distant, unfeeling body. In *The Men*, Brando's paraplegic is more or less pushed into the world of the normals by his own needs and through the encouragement of the character played by Theresa Wright, the girl he had left behind. Outside of the doctor's lecture to the wives and girl friends of paraplegics on whether or not they can father children, there is little in the film to suggest sexual struggle and absolutely nothing to suggest the possibility of sexual joy. Even the opposition of the two women actresses, the tight, virtually sexless Theresa Wright and the hesitantly giving Jane Fonda, points up the contrast.

But it is not the choice of the paraplegic as hero that dictates such contrasts; rather, it is the time and the audience for which these two films were made. *The Men* was created for a nation which had just emerged from World War II and which viewed itself as a just, solid society trying to get back to traditional virtues. It is easy, but not particularly fair, to ridicule that America along with the simple pieties it claimed as its own. Our inheritance today is comprised of different myths, but different myths simply indicate different realities facing us. There was still a line of relationship between Deerslayer and Brando in *The Men*. In our time, that line has been broken, a fact that is evident not only in the pacifism that *Coming Home* endorses but in its conceptions of freedom and sexuality, too. Even Hollywood seems to have learned that what counts is what men do with their fates. The movement now is away from genital sexuality and towards a complex sensuality; we insist now that a man's freedom is more important than his need to identify that freedom for others. And this freedom is not captured through inner tensions but through a simple acquiescence to circumstance, a way in which a man comes to know himself and emerges a better man.

It is not by accident that the western as a film genre seems all but dead, and that the cult of machismo in film can now be given life only through parody.[7] Hollywood can tinker with a "more realistic" manhood, it can romanticize the very qualities it has put forward as "natural" to the new film hero. After all, it is the nature of Hollywood to try to cheat at what it depicts. For all of its skillful manipulation of the viewer's sympathies, *Coming Home* is a less honest film than *The Men*. It lacks a commitment to the felt experience, and it avoids the pain and humiliation that one must push through in order to become a man. Nonetheless, it seems to me a healthy step forward for a culture in which men have traditionally been seen as either "hard" or "soft," "weak" or "strong," "manly" or "effeminate." The emotional adequacy of manhood is no trifling theme, even when approached by Hollywood. And if, as I believe, the imaginations of men feed the movies, then men have at last begun to emerge from their long isolation.

FOOTNOTES

1. John Updike, *Bech: A Book* (New York, 1970), pp. 5–6.

2. Michael Wood, *America in the Movies* (New York, 1975), pp. 192–193. These past two decades have produced a staggering bibliography on film. Having worked through a great deal of this material, let me note here the books I found particularly useful: Michael Wood's book is a humorous, dispassionate inquiry into what Hollywood did to us and what we, in turn, did to Hollywood; *Man and the Movies* is an interesting collection of essays edited by W. R. Robinson; and Molly Haskell's study of the treatment of women in the movies, *From Reverence to Rape*, deserves the high praise it has received. One wonders why no one has yet done a similar analysis of Hollywood's treatment of men.

3. Larry McMurtry, "Cowboys, Movies, Myths, and Cadillacs: Realism in the Western," in *Man and the Movies*, ed. W. R. Robinson (Baltimore, 1969), p. 48.

4. Henry Bamford Parkes, "Metamorphoses of Leatherstocking," in *Literature in America*, ed. Philip Rahv (New York, 1957), pp. 436–437.

5. Molly Haskell, *From Reverence to Rape: The Treatment of Women in the Movies* (New York, 1974), p. 358.

6. Paul Starr, "Hollywood's New Ideal of Masculinity," *The New York Times*, "Arts and Leisure" (July 16, 1978), p. 1.

7. This accounts for the success of Burt Reynolds in films such as *Gator, The Longest Yard,* and *Hooper.* Reynolds has created a formula in which machismo is parodied in the very creation, so that the audience is able to laugh at it and to desire it at one and the same time. The masculine ideal of an older type reemerges even as he is the object of laughter.

Chapter Seven
The Homosexual as Other

From my car window, I see a black man in a blue and white jogging suit who is coaching a group of black children between the ages of eight and eleven in an after-school recreation program. The children are jogging slowly around the quarter-mile track. "One more!" the man cries out, clapping his hands together. "One more lap!" He pauses, eyes the unenthusiastic kids, who move slowly, bundled together in a pack. "Last one home is a faggot!" he screams angrily.

They react as if they have been kicked. The pack breaks apart, the stronger runners pushing to the front. The kids run desperately, straining against their own endurance. A lean young girl with long legs bursts to the head of the group. As she crosses the finish line, she cries out triumphantly, "I ain't no fuckin' faggot!" The last runner to cross the line is a very fat boy. His tits jiggle like a girl just past pubescence, his jowled face is crestfallen. I wonder whether he is going to cry. But I turn the ignition key in my car and do not wait to find out.

I

As children, we did not so much learn the alternatives as absorb them. They floated in the very air we breathed: man or faggot, those who fucked and those who were fucked. And no matter how willing we may be today to set such collective childhood delusions onto the scale weighing reality, the homosexual alternative still remains a particularly difficult reality to encompass. We are judgemental—and we are judgemental about nothing so much as about the quality of our manhood. We remember the game called Kick a Queer in the Teeth. The price derived was the collective manhood of the pack—beating up that which might look like you, move like you, even talk like you, but that which you knew was the very antithesis of the man you were on the verge of becoming. But even the heterosexual who is beyond the cruelty of adolescent queer-baiting is wary of the territory homosexuals occupy. It is, after all, not his—and he knows that it is not the territory of manhood. If as children, none of us was quite certain of what it was homosexuals actually *did,* we knew enough to damn the difference anyway.

As men, we simply took what the child had absorbed and denied its complexity. We could fit the stories we heard—how X had returned from the army queer, how Y was rumored to be making it both ways—into the world we saw. The *threat* of homosexuality, if *threat* is the word that describes the distance we meant to keep between *us* and *them,* was not so much of what it was *they* did (by this time we knew) but of the element of parody that hunched within their differences from us. For heterosexuals in the 1950s, the homosexual was a man who actively mocked his own manhood. We believed—indeed, it was inevitable that we believe—that a man *chose* to be a homosexual in much the same manner as he chose to dress in a particular style. The belief was reinforced by psychoanalysis and law and by virtually all the other institutions of the culture. And the belief made it that much easier to insist that homosexuality was a negation of manhood. It also made it that much more difficult to look upon the demands of organized homosexuals with the same kind of sympathy and admiration that one looked upon the demands of women and blacks. Not that the homosexual demands were more threatening, nor that they were demands that would force a man to face, as so many homosexuals wanted to believe, the secret homosexual lurking within himself.[1] The demands of women were much more unsettling to the sexual balance of power and to the status of men, while the demands of blacks certainly wreaked more havoc with the white American man's political power. Despite Kinsey and his statistics, homosexuality was peripheral to the world of most American men.

But when homosexuals insisted on making themselves models of a manhood we believed they could merely parody, heterosexual men in this country were faced with a problem they still cannot handle successfully. For the homosexual claim in this country today is very close to the claims made by men we have traditionally admired. In the act of seizing control of his own fate, of insisting on *his* right to define the world that he sees according to those insights he has acquired as a homosexual, he presents us with his conception of what a man is. And he tells us that he possesses the very thing that we lack—reliance on his own ability to face the world as it is, and to face it without deceit or hypocrisy. *Macho* connotes a style that we can no longer believe in, but the need to live honestly still commands admiration.

The homosexual now demands admiration from other American men, something we are having difficulty granting. And yet, he is doing what we cannot do. And he is asking us to look on his homosexuality simply as that which he is fated to live with. To be a homosexual, he is saying, is not to be any less of a man. If the price demanded for his manhood is that he come out of the closet, well, then, he is going to pay that price. And exactly what do we heterosexuals have to match that?

The chief demand militant homosexuals make of the world is that they be free from outside definition. They actively resist the fate others have meted out to them. And the problem heterosexual men have with this, and the reason, I suspect, why we remain so ill at ease with the Gay Liberation Movement as a movement, is that it threatens so many of the myths to which our lives have been anchored. If not even a faggot is a faggot, and if in our society the faggots are no longer willing to permit themselves to be kicked in the teeth, then exactly where does that leave heterosexual men who seem so willing to be kicked by anyone at all?

By living consciously with his own reality, the homosexual creates out of his life that very resistance to the limitations of existence which one learns to admire in others. He matches the man within to the reality he embraces. Is not this exactly what the cripple does? And does it not, ultimately, lead to the belief that the quality of one's manhood is better because the conditions combating it are stronger, more oppressive, than those the normal has to face? The homosexual must constantly measure up, even when he denies the rights of others to create the standards of measurement. In Marcel Orphuls' superb documentary about France under the Nazis, *The Sor-*

row and the Pity, there is a moving scene in which an obviously homosexual Englishman is questioned about his
wartime activities with the Resistance in France. The inter-
view takes place in his home, where he sits surrounded by his
plants and his cats—a quiet, domesticated existence. In a shy,
almost virginal voice he speaks about why he did what he did,
confessing that as a homosexual he felt that he had to prove
to himself that he was as brave, as manly, as other men; thar
he had, in short, the right to call himself a man.

But it has always been the *heterosexual* who demanded the
right to call himself a man, who made his distinctions about
the world on that basis alone. We live with a peculiar reversal
today. We heterosexuals are the ones who are unsure of ourselves and of who we are; we are the ones who pull back into
a self-effacing defensiveness in our relations with the outside
world. We lack purpose, are no longer certain of what we are
supposed to be nor of our ability to become anything at all.
We have a sense of dislocation, of being excluded from a
game in which the players make up the rules as they go along.
We suspect that we are in the process of losing out in the very
races we once called our own.

And we have seen others over whom we once assumed
superiority come forward to stake their claims: blacks who
now insist that we are not as good as their ambition has made
them, women who claim that they are tougher and more
courageous and able to endure pain better than we can. But
the alternative that most decisively offends the myths we
have been brought up to embrace is the homosexual: *He* can
now insist on his right to be what he is while we scurry from
one idea to the other seeking a usable self. This may be the
most ironic of commentaries on the present condition of men
in our society. For in claiming to admire those who seize the
moment offered them, we find ourselves now being asked to
consider the claim of those whose manhood we had once so
casually been able to dismiss.

II

THERE IS SOMETHING EPICENE about him—a soft inside that
fills out the space it occupies. I have worked with him occasionally in the faculty anti-war movement and in one or two
other causes. But he irritates me all the same. He seems so
disembodied, so rooted to the abstractions of the sociology he
teaches and the slogans he voices. As I enter the faculty
dining room, I see him sitting at a table along with my friend,
M., and two students, both women. M. waves as I walk inside
the crowded room and points to the empty chair at their
table. I reluctantly head for it. I like M., but I am not particularly eager to join the students or the sociologist. I approach the table intent on pushing the irritation in me to the
point where it can command. I sit down. The sociologist
greets me, introduces me to the two students in that late-
sixties academic style, all first names and smiling teeth. He
annoys me; I turn to M.

The talk at the table is desultory until at last the sociologist
removes an envelope of photographs from the briefcase at his
feet. He smiles at the two students, then spreads the photographs on the table before us. "The march last week," he
explains. "For Gay Rights." He points to a photograph of a
bearded man holding up one side of a banner. "That's me."
The girls stare at the pictures, then smile. They cannot show
surprise. M.'s face is a blank. In any case, the revelation
cannot have been startling to any of us. As he shows us the
pictures like a tourist trying to recapture a Roman spring, his
homosexuality seems absorbed into the soft lines of his life.
My irritation grows. In 1969, defining oneself outside ordinary society was more done than not. And although I cannot
yet admit to the idea that homosexuality can offer itself as a
political proposition, as I watch the eyes of the students fill
with confused distance, I discover that I feel a certain grudging admiration for him. He is not unaware of the price he

must pay. Until this point I had thought of him as lacking an inner life.

He is fired from the college the following semester. But not for the sin of having come out in public; rather, he is too radical, caught in the shrinkage of the sixties. He gets a job in California, but he can think only of his coming out. Occasionally, I hear about him from M. or from another friend with whom he continues a correspondence. The letters slack off as he moves deeper into the homosexual world. He gives up research in sociology, moves away from academia. Now he insists he is interested only in the self's knowledge of its own validity. Until his emergence in public as a homosexual, he writes M., he had never known the name of anyone he had made love to. In my mind, I picture that short epicene body with the frightened quizzical eyes and I am struck once again by the extent to which men make their sexuality into their myths. A year later he is fired from the California post, this time for good. In an article he publishes in a radical sociological review, he dismisses the academic world. He has better things to do with his time. He is now absolutely intent on creating meaning for his life as a homosexual, having discovered in the Gay Movement both sexuality and solidarity, a sense of purpose as an individual. In the past he was a prisoner of the idea of manhood. Now he writes that he is determined "to struggle against it . . . to keep from being mutilated out of all human shape." He is determined to live honestly; he insists that only by acknowledging his homosexuality as the essence of his being can he function honestly in this world.

And yet, the struggle never ends. Manhood is aggression, he insists. "I am not now, nor have I ever been, a man," he writes, as if denial eliminated the condition. Coming out has convinced him that if he denies the actuality he can deny that he is subject to the need. He wants nothing less than to make courage out of absence. He drifts from one gay commune to the next. He captures one lover after the next, seeking what both homosexuals and heterosexuals call "a lasting relationship." Defining himself out of manhood, he discovers that world in which to be a homosexual is by definition to be a revolutionary. In pushing against manhood, he believes that he is fighting all forms of oppression—capitalism, the state, technological power, the need to be defined by any outside force. He aims to meld into a collective of his peers, his sexual partners. But the difficulties overwhelm him. He now defines himself as pure sexual being. He is the creature of his own needs. In a letter written late in 1976, he speaks of the latest lover, who has spurned his advances because he does not like the sociologist's fat, soft body. As soon as he learns to love his own body, he writes, he will be able to. . . .

All around him, the forces gather. Losing weight for the lover who spurned him, he tries to turn back to Marxism, to the brave new world in which men will finally rid themselves of those qualities they have always associated with manhood. The barriers between brothers will fall, institutions will no longer oppress, life will stretch out before him like a chain in which all bodies will be suitably bound to all lovers, a frieze as immortal as that on Keats' Grecian urn.

In one of his final letters, he writes, "I want to exterminate all vestiges of manhood in myself." But he still complains that his body is not yet appealing to his lover. The idea of getting beyond manhood constantly forces him into a sexual role, but he must learn to live with this paradox. He wants so much *not* to be a man that he parodies subservience, chokes off his intelligence, his sensitivity, even his longing to get beyond the sexual.

He kills himself in 1978. No one knows why. He leaves no notes, no explanations. *I want to exterminate all vestiges of manhood in myself.* He succeeds, finally, in exterminating the self.

III

I HAVE QUITE CONSCIOUSLY FORCED THE ROLE of representative homosexual upon the sociologist. Examples tend to deny complexity and difference. And I do continue to see homosexuality as a denial of the continuity that I seek in manhood, although I acknowledge that this denial takes many different forms. From the leather-jacketed toughs who patrol Christopher Street like gangster princes to the elderly men who walk arm-in-arm through Central Park, the styles are complex. And so, quite obviously, are the lives. One does not have to read the many books about the homosexual situation to recognize that the population by and large reflects the larger heterosexual community. This group is not motivated by love or by fear or by crusading, but, as is the case with most groups, it is in large part motivated by the self-interest of its members.

Even as one discovers that he has to admire in homosexuals what he admires in others—the demand that the world accept them as they are—he also comes to understand that their particular forms of defiance still stand at some distance from the political. As a whole, the style of the Gay Revolution seems to stress a kind of self-centered hedonism which fits in very well with what we see in heterosexual culture. The lover who refused the sociologist because he disliked his body is closer to our own reality *and* the homosexual's reality than the Marx who wanted to redeem man by destroying competition. The question one asks over and over of the homosexual defiance of heterosexual society is whether the self facing its inner truths can, through its difference, establish the presence it desires. Behind a good deal of the rhetoric of homosexuality lurks the very element which binds the homosexual to his heterosexual judge—the need to prove that his being is complete, that he is capable of accepting any challenge.

The effort to escape from the limitations of manhood becomes a parody of manhood. In a homosexual waterfront bar,
men stick their cocks through holes drilled in toilet partitions
in the effort to become the hero touching his fate, awaiting
the answer to the question of whether one is brave enough or
desperate enough to take this chance, too. In much the same
manner, I suspect, men once risked the unknown on the
assumption that only in risk was man alive. And yet, one
wonders whether the homosexual who goes to the hole again
and again, testing the expectation of orifice unattached to any
form other than orifice unattached to form and then thrusts
himself home is merely riding on the motions of his own
desperation. One wonders too whether he is any more to be
called to judgement than his heterosexual brother who has
cut himself off from the contact of sex, for whom the bodies
are names, the faces beyond seeing, the orgasms hoarded like
copper pennies. Beneath all difference, ultimate similarities:
A hole is a hole. And so much of substance can be risked for a
promise that is anonymous, unremitting, absolute only in its
negation of the self.

"No individual is limited," wrote Freud, "to the modes of
reaction of a single sex but always finds some room for those
of the opposite one." Couched in such clinical terms, one's
tolerance can easily be granted. But we are always being
pulled up short by the myths of our pasts. The homosexual
intent on the legitimacy of his personal liberation is obliged to
show himself to our eyes as the last true believer in the
transforming power of love: We insist that he service the
romantic in us. Otherwise, it would be difficult to recognize
in the homosexual those very qualities the heterosexual admires: the search for an integral self, the insistence that no
outside force has the right to classify what one is. How much
better the word *courage* sounds in Hemingway than it does in
Genet.

A poet friend tells me of a visit to a gay religious service in
his housing complex; he tries to assume a tolerant neutrality.

But he acknowledges that he is uncomfortable all through the service. There is something wrong; the dimensions of his reality have been twisted out of shape. He is apologetic in speaking about it. Like me, he does not want to condemn, is afraid even to hint that he still believes theirs is a lesser manhood.

"I don't really understand it," he says. "I'm past all that queer-baiting. Still, you watch men gather together like that and you find that you're terribly ill at ease. I didn't want to be—I'm angry at myself for feeling that way." I suspect that my own reaction would be the same. I would be disappointed in myself for not measuring up to my beliefs, disappointed in the homosexuals for not realizing that imitation is parody. Despite my recognition that we take our examples of living where we can, the condition still irritates me. I want to admire the homosexual other, if admire I must, from a distance. I am irritated by the very heaviness of the responsibility, the way it seems so total in the lives of the few homosexuals I know.

The time of Kick a Queer in the Teeth is over—and over, we must remind ourselves, because the much-despised queers started kicking back—but the sense of distance between *them* and *us* is almost as wide as it was. One would think we might finally have learned to live with the honesty of those who choose to emerge from where they were hiding. But we haven't. We can accept a heterosexual sexuality that employs every conceivable demonstration of prowess that our sexual mechanics can facilitate, yet we remain ill at ease when faced with the homosexual other.

To leave it at that would be too simple. I must make an observation that seems endemic to the reality of homosexuality: that the homosexual parodies so many of the elements in the culture which he claims to deny, that in the very effort to capture a "normalcy" he imposes a definition of himself which makes the accident of his homosexuality into the core of his reality. There is something brave in choosing to come out, but there is something here that pulls existence out of all proportion, too. All too often, the act of coming out becomes a substitute for the need to win a self.

IV

HE USED TO LIVE NEAR US, and when I meet him again on a visit to see his parents I remember how I would watch him silently struggle then with all his difficult possibilities. We shake hands; I ask him how he is doing. He tells me he has just graduated from college. And then he says, "I'm gay now." There is something simple and clear in the confession. He wants this honesty between us, and he says it as if he were telling me that he was about to go off to law school or had decided to pursue a career as a veterinarian. His is, ultimately, a domesticated courage, but he is still sufficiently unsure of it to want to justify himself. For what is he telling me—that he has the right *to be*, simply to be? He is claiming his right to a passport that will enable him to accept the condition.

In the long run, this right will serve as an advantage—not that he is now a man of courage but that he can feel himself a man. *I'm gay now.* A simple statement, but a coup in a world where to define oneself as anything at all is considered a virtue. He has caught a glimpse of himself, and for perhaps the first time in his life it is a self about which he does not have to feel ambivalent. He is saying that he has been bullied long enough, and he will no longer join in the bullying himself.

The homosexual insists that he is now the man in whom the need to transcend the definition imposed by his culture has given shape to his life. And there is a legitimate advantage he can claim. He is not a hero; he is certainly not a model of manhood for heterosexuals; he can be as mendacious and preening as one can imagine—but *he is.* In a culture which once refused to look at him, or else used his existence as a form of comic relief, the fact that the homosexual has made others aware of his personal rights is a triumph. While other men struggle with the need to define themselves through strategies considered acceptable by society, the homosexual believes that he has now forged a consistent view of himself and made that view understandable to society. The fact that he presents himself as a man rather than as a victim may be, to heterosexual eyes, his greatest sin. He assumes that his boundaries are no narrower than our own, while his expectations of life are as great as ours. As far as he is concerned, his life is as worthy of emulation as any other.

And yet, even as we recognize this, we continue to see him as the man who has denied the man in himself. His presence makes us uncomfortable because it goes against the grain of everything we have been taught about manhood, about survival, on acceptable terms. He parodies the domestic arrangements of our lives.[2] The screaming faggot is not the one who poses the challenge to our lives, but rather it is the shy hero in *The Sorrow and the Pity* and the elderly couples who dote on one another in their version of domesticated tranquillity that disturb our conceptions of our own superiority. They violate our sense of order, not our sense of biology. It is not that we heterosexuals believe that men cannot touch one another or that they cannot show mutual affection. No, it is, rather, that the clichés we still cannot quite face up to are designed to maintain that distance between them and us.

If we look truthfully and honestly at both them and us, however, I suspect that we will see that if manhood is to be reclaimed we are going to have to match the homosexual's willingness to live with what he is with our own willingness. And in a culture in which most of us believe deep down that a homosexual is nothing but a man who has broken under the weight of manhood, that is going to be as difficult a task as we have yet faced.

FOOTNOTES

1. "You run away from the homosexual that is you," says Denise to Sergius at the end of Mailer's "The Time of Her Time." It is a line that embodies the attitude of the fifties to homosexuality. Against this, our contemporary view that the homosexual is, as Kate Millett writes, "our current 'nigger' of love."

2. The theme is remarkably presented in Hubert Selby Jr.'s *Last Exit to Brooklyn*. In a less violent form, it also appears in many homosexual confessionals designed to show that the homosexual is just like everybody else—only more so.

Chapter Eight
The Black Alternative

LULA: *Don't think you'll get out of your responsibility that way. It's not cold at all. You Fascist! Into my dark living room. Where we'll sit and talk endlessly, endlessly.*
CLAY: *About what?*
LULA: *About what? About your manhood, what do you think? What do you think we've been talking about all this time?*

—*LeRoi Jones,* Dutchman

But the contemporary black man no longer exists for his people or even for himself. He has made himself a living testament to the white man's failures. He must continue to suffer, to be brutalized, and to brutalize his peers until whites are able to become the better people that will be required to deliver him from his condition. He has become a martyr. And he has arrived in this place, not because of the dependency inflicted upon him in slavery, but because his black perspective, like the white perspective, supported the notion that manhood is more valuable than anything else.

—*Michele Wallace,* Black Macho and
the Myth of the Superwoman

I

"WE SHALL HAVE OUR MANHOOD," cried Eldridge Cleaver. "We shall have it or the earth will be leveled by our attempts to gain it." This demand embarrasses us today, forces us back into a time whose very innocence may prove its ultimate gift: the idea that men might will manhood into being, that one group of men might, in defining their own collective black consciousness for America, help the American white man define his manhood, too. It was, god knows, a short-lived dream, doomed as much by the imposition of one pigmentation on manhood as it was by the insistence that men could limit themselves exclusively to racial bonding. And yet, how does one speak about what black men have brought to the American scene over the past two decades? So much has been written about the black man's relation to white American society that one inevitably approaches the subject with a sigh of exasperation and considerable trepidation. It all seems so clear—the black man declaring himself a man, his positioning himself beyond the boundaries of white America, his growing contempt for the styles of masculine reality that white Americans have apparently embraced, his struggling to achieve a sense of realistic terms and possible new ventures in which *his* manhood, as *he* defines it, becomes the gauge by which others measure their own adequacy as men.

I have no intention of adding my voice to that grating

cacophony of whites trying to "explain" themselves to blacks, so heavily laden with guilt that they are willing to make themselves ludicrous as they swell the chorus of *mea culpa.* But the territory must be covered, for this is a book about manhood in American life. And blacks have certainly made their presence felt there.

In the early 1960s, as the Civil Rights movement gathered momentum, black men in America stated that their manhood was as good as that of whites. Simply to exist as a black man in America was to have proved one's mettle, to have come through against the most formidable odds. Given the stress under which they had to carve out an identiy, it was probably inevitable that the demand for equality was soon transformed into the idea that black men could evoke a masculine authority that was racial rather than personal. And as resistance to their demands for equality continued, black men began to assume an image in which black was not *equal to* but *bigger than* white. As the sixties moved into the seventies, black men were saying that they were tougher and braver and nastier and subtler than their white counterparts, that a black man ate and drank and fucked and blew music and drove and boxed and ran and played football and baseball and basketball and even breathed in a way that his white counterpart could not emulate—and that being the case, why, then, it followed that he was more the man of the two.

Admittedly, it is not a new argument. The history of relationships between groups seems to repeat itself endlessly. From time before recorded history, men have been hammering out these dull-witted racial and religious and ethnic superiorities on each other's bodies and minds. Even though the results of such claims never seem to be useful for very long, one must take these competitive comparisons seriously. They certainly deserve a place in examining the reality of black history in America. For more than any other group in this nation—more than homosexuals, more than Jews, more than women—blacks have been defined by others. And it has been a definition in which the centrality of race has been affirmed by white America.[1]

Today, too, the current black stance is that the black man's tragic history is not really the element with which whites have to be concerned. For blacks, the crux of the problem remains what the white man is doing to himself. And there is still a suspicion on the part of both whites and blacks that the reason for the ascendency of black manhood is the growing retreat of white men from the possibilities and privileges that once dominated their lives. Black men are apparently more willing than whites to live with the idea of manhood as a crucial presence directing their energies.[2] Having in the past been deprived of the challenge and consolation of the ascendency of manhood, blacks now seem to have taken it upon themselves to embrace the very ideals that helped contribute to their misery. Having believed for so long that they had been "emasculated" by white men who fought to protect what they had neither earned nor hungered after, blacks discovered that the rewards of manhood in America were substantial.

"Husband and father, lover and master, breadwinner and decision-maker—these roles were not traps to him but the belated triumphs of centuries. After three hundred years, he was at last throwing off the long slavery of caste, at last learning what it meant to live as a man. The word was no joke to him. He had been a 'boy' too long to fail to honor it."[3] How ironic that the black challenge, probably the most irritating of all challenges to traditional conceptions of American manhood, was not issued in the name of change (which is what both feminists and homosexuals were demanding) but on the basis of how well one performed at being a man. In essence, blacks have demanded of whites that they demonstrate that they are as good as they claim to be, that they deserve the superiority they have assumed. A good deal of this is no more than a kind of hyperbolic gamesmanship. But realistically, there is something to be said for the black argument.

The black man remains as split by the body/mind dichotomy as anyone else in America. For he discovers that in the very act of giving vent to his rage and anger, in affirming his virility, his sense of himself as man, he backs away from his own mind. Men face their realities through language. But a language geared to the centrality of one's color is a language that mocks the very reality it claims to seize. One of the most interesting aspects of *The Autobiography of Malcolm X* is Malcolm's didactic, at times even pompous, belief in the power of language to persuade and to revivify. The chapter in *The Autobiography* in which the transformation affected by language and intellect is most deeply felt deals with Malcolm X's conversion to the religion of Islam. It also deals with his newly discovered literacy, which bursts forth as an uncontrolled voracious appetite. Its very confusions of intellect and color—"Spinoza impressed me for a while when I found out he was black"—highlight the extent to which a man's view of his own mind can be crippled. Nonetheless, the chapter is as powerful a tribute to the transformation accomplished by the mind as anything else I know.

The trap closes on the black man at the very moment he sees himself emerging as a measuring gauge of American manhood. Centering his image around his willingness to take risks, he finds that he is both victim and perpetrator of his authority. For the only superiority the white world can be persuaded to grant him is the power of his body. And that power proves to be tenuous and short-lived. A man's body is as much subject to definition from outside as is his mind. And the black man remains the victim of myths—damned if he defines himself in their terms and damned if he refuses. Even in the midst of taking what it has been denied, the black legacy is informed of its limits. In no other group has the assertion of manhood been so fundamentally a Catch-22 situation. Attempts to replace the political rhetoric of the 1960s with an analysis anchored to the everyday realities of black life seem to have met with little success. Should black men join the American middle class, the sociologists ponder? One wonders just what his own reaction to the conflict would be. One is still left with the black man defined by others, and defined, almost invariably, in terms of his body. The black man is placed in the insane position of having to prove he is "nigger" enough for the white world, an idea that was forcefully explored in *Dutchman.*

> LULA: [*Becoming annoyed that he will not dance, and becoming more animated as if to embarrass him still further*]
>
> Come on, Clay . . . let's do the thing. Uhh! Uhh! Clay! Clay! You middle-class black bastard. Forget your social-working mother for a few seconds and let's knock stomachs. Clay, you liver-lipped white man. You would-be Christian. You ain't no nigger, you're just a dirty white man. Get up, Clay. Dance with me, Clay.[4]

Clay cannot defend his manhood from Lula's devastating knife. After all, the world has turned on him before and there is no reason to believe it will not do so again.

II

THE ADVANTAGE THAT BLACKS seemed to have over whites in the 1960s was their ability to muster a great deal of energy in the service of racial pride. It was, as Cleaver and others put it, the primacy of their "manhood" that was at stake, and they would have to wrest it from white America. But in the 1970s, the quality of that manhood blacks had been demanding began to dissolve into mere rhetoric. This is certainly the charge that informs the recent book by Michele Wallace, a black feminist who indicates that black women feel less than that "gender euphoria" Natalie Gittelson speaks of in *Dominus*. The argument seems to lie at the heart of the attention black men have paid to the need for an affirmative sense of what manhood can deliver. For Wallace, black macho is a perpetuation of male adolescence which has placed an intolerable burden on black women; for Ms. Gittelson, the "gender euphoria" of black men had at its core the sense of masculinity as a spendable currency that had all but disappeared from the young white world. The real black conception of manhood probably lies somewhere between the two.

In the late 1960s and the early 1970s, black male students in college seemed considerably more definitive in their conceptions of themselves and in their ideas of what a man should be than their white counterparts. Manhood was for blacks what it had been for whites—a balancing act between the self and the outside world as well as between different facets of the self. But there was a new ease for most black men in accomplishing this act. It was not that blacks knew what profession or occupation they wanted to enter any better than whites did. But they *did* know that a man advanced his specific individual claims against the world. And they seemed considerably less afraid of that world than whites. For most of my black college students, there was a clear pleasure in a man's very existence.

That pleasure has all but evaporated as we approach the 1980s. Like their white peers, the black college students I teach are victims of shrivelled times and expectations. The political climate no longer supports them, and talk of "black power" and "black is beautiful" is a mere mockery of the past; ideology seems thin and blacks find themselves bound to the problems and dilemmas of their white counterparts. The question is not merely how to get a job or choose the right profession; it is, rather, the more difficult question of what it is to be a man. Superfly now wants not a revolution but the security of bourgeois solidity, a "nine-to-five job with a decent future," as my students remind me. It is an honorable ambition, the same kind that motivated whites who once stepped furtively into the larger world from their provincial streets and towns. But it is not the kind of ambition that supplies manhood, or establishes that sense of daring and combat which sets one man apart from his fellows. Black men discover that they are no longer outlaws and they are no longer models: Instead they are the guardians of that very respectability whites have been yearning to give up.

Perhaps the chief reason for the failure of the black man to continue as an alternative model for American manhood is that he has been forced to come to terms with the limited success that life promises him. He must make the same choices that white men before him have made: He must decide between a physical self that satisfies his desire for a heroic image and a working self that functions in terms of what men actually do to make their way through this world. As long as the black man could take the risk of gambling with odds so strongly stacked against him, he could look on his life from a distance. The essence of "cool" came from separating the self from what threatened the self. One could do one's own choosing, decide which risks were worth taking and which were not. In this manner, the black man, possessor of a certain cachet, could establish an enviable presence in American life.

But the manhood blacks offered America during the 1960s seems limited today *because* it was so traditionally American, affirming those very qualities white American men wanted to give up, the renewed recognition that one's manhood was not a gift bestowed by others but rather something the individual forced others to recognize. In trying to impose manhood by the physical reality of their bodies, black men discovered that they had limited their own scope.

They were correct in understanding that manhood could be

formed only in opposition to the pieties and thin quiescences of the past, in opposition to resignation and sufferance. As they looked around themselves in the 1960s, they discovered that whites were trapped within something every bit as spiritually demeaning as the ghetto, a society which made it overwhelmingly difficult to be a man because it so severely limited the important testing grounds. Whites, for the most part, drifted through crises because there was little against which they could prove their manhood and affirm their existences. Although the black alternative of creating manhood out of limitation might not have pushed very far beyond past conceptions of what the black man was, it was still one of the few affirmations of manhood that one could find in the 1960s. Manhood, blacks assumed, could only grow out of active resistance to whatever tried to confine it, and this is a valuable lesson, one that all men must continue to absorb. In a world increasingly devoid of the authority of example, perhaps the best men can still hope for is the courage to create a sense of manhood out of their own condition.

III

I AM FOURTEEN YEARS OLD and twice a week I am ferried down to the Hospital for Joint Diseases at Madison Avenue and 124th Street for hydrotherapy. As I wait for the station wagon that is to take me home, I pretend that the territory surrounding the hospital is dangerous. But this is only a game I play. The black faces that surround me on these streets are passive, removed. I remember the three or four black boys I have known in the hospital. Lifeless legs, lifeless arms, the deadness of time on their hands.

I have an hour to kill before the station wagon picks me up

and so I make my way haltingly to Mount Morris Park across the street. It is a warm, sun-filled April day. I sit in the park among a few scattered winos and old people passing the time. I do not want to believe that I am like them and so I close my eyes and dream dreams of power, of prowess. I snatch at images, trying to rid myself of the humiliating resentment of having had my lifeless legs manipulated in the hot pool by the physical therapist. I fantasize about her. She is remarkably beautiful, a red-haired tawny-skinned woman whom I want with the mingled sexual anxiety of the adolescent and the cripple.

In two more years I will explode into a willed self-rehabilitation which will do more for me than any hydrotherapy. But now I dream my dreams. I fuck through my adolescent fears and I am whole again. I clothe myself in fantasy, sniff the spring air, and play centerfield for the Brooklyn Dodgers. I would gladly give up endurance (which I already sense is the only thing that can save me) for wholeness, which is simpler. In my dream self, the crutches drift into invisibility. I race through time, alive, sharp with the sense of onrushing fulfillment. Until the smell of sour wine breath and rotting gums pulls me back to reality. Eyes still closed, I hear, "They got you." Slurred voice to match the breath. "They done you bad, man." I have lost the sweets of the dream but I fight to keep my eyes closed because I can imagine the face all too vividly—the eyes red-splotched and bleary, like those of a dying man, all awareness slipped into the corners of the eyes. I do not want to give him my moment. I struggle against it, but I cannot get away from him. I know that I am going to open my eyes and give him the victory. And I do. I see the real face, looking exactly as I had imagined it, and I think, *black son of a bitch, I'd like to cut your heart out.* Instead, I smile politely. "Who?" I ask.

He laughs. "They done you, buddy," he insists. "Don't shit

me. I sees what I sees. Man, they done you good." He palms
the bottle of wine in his hand, not even in a paper bag but
naked in his large pink palm. I shake my head. I am furious.
He shrugs, trying to be generous. "You just a boy," he says.
"Ain't nothin' but a boy." He swallows a long draught of the
wine, leans back into the bench, belches. "Shit, that don't
matter. They done you anyway."

I am angry, self-righteous. "Listen," I want to say,"you
don't understand. There's nothing personal to it. You just get
sick. That's all. It's not like being black. You think like that,
you think someone has done something to you, and you'll go
crazy." But I remain silent, examining his face. It is a face
that tells me what his survival as a man has cost him. And
others. It grates against the beliefs I have learned to cherish,
even at fourteen. There is nothing noble about it. It is the face
of a man whose only accomplishment has been survival. *I
have survived*, the face says, *fuck you.*

Trying to get by, trying to maneuver to the park bench and
take whatever there is to take. He needs what I need, but at
fourteen I cannot admit that—not to him, not to myself. He
smells of wine and dirt. He is an alien in the rich fat of
America. Even in this battle-scarred Harlem, he is an alien.
Are they, in the hospital across the street, noting the bleary-
eyed wino on the park bench who is convinced in his thickening wine-sodden paranoia that *they,* the world's minions,
have done this to him? And to me? Only by existing does
black remain black. It is that simple.

But I am different. I know that I am. I do not want to be
anything less than a man in this America. I do not want this
black wino as a model for destiny nor the special sufferance
his red eyes and dulled sensibilities tell me he considers my
due as well as his. I do not want his drunken insistence on
community, his battered body rehearsing the roles we can
feed each other. Manhood escapes victimization, even at four-

teen. Somewhere within me, though, I begin to wonder whether he has not outlined my condition better than anyone else can. He may know me better than I am prepared to know myself. He, too, has left the world of the normals; he, too, knows that the only chance he has to reclaim the man within is to hammer away at what he believes *they* have done. And it may be that his greatest advantage is that he can assume *they* have done it. He will delude himself, but he will not lie.

His is an alternative manhood, a harsh bitter one that sustains itself through the dips and ends of survival. "Look," he is saying to me, "you never going to play ball again, you never going to fuck like a normal, you never going to run on no goddamned Hollywood dipped-in-shit-kiss-my-ass beach, you never going to. . . ." And I can fill in the blanks. Labels, roles. Quiet panic rising from the gut.

Could I live with that? All of it? Taking only what was available? Fear, guilt, anxiety. Like a black man. Like a faggot. Like the cripple I was. To hell with it. I could not get off the world. I wasn't brave enough for that. All that was left was to create my life. Manhood was still out of my grasp, unless I was willing to settle for mere survival. My dreams would not hold up, although my anger would. Murder and rage might drift through a man's heart, but if he managed to get past them for a moment, then perhaps he could get beyond them permanently. What, I wonder now, would I have done with the image of myself struggling on the beach at Noordwijk had I been able to envision it at fourteen, sitting on a park bench next to a black wino?

I get up and, haltingly, I move away. The wino waves, not nearly so intent on my retreating form as I want to believe. I see the station wagon waiting for me at the entrance to the hospital's out-patient wing. I do not even mind when the sallow-faced driver complains of having had to wait.

I get into the station wagon, drop my crutches to the floor, then pull my brace-bound legs after me. When we turn north on the corner of Madison, I glance across at the park bench where the wino is still sitting, still oblivious—as much of a man among men as his daring will allow him to be. Not you, I think, I'll do better. But I am not really certain that I can.

FOOTNOTES

1. The reception of *The Autobiography of Malcolm X* is a paradigm of the problems facing the black man in America when he tries to create and sustain a selfhood independent of white America. It is one thing to claim, as Malcolm does, that such a selfhood can only exist independent of the judgement of white America; it is quite another to remove oneself from the strains of the world one lives in by making race the only thing to which a man is responsible. How many of us have been so impressed by the quality of voice in Malcolm's *Autobiography* that we were quite willing to overlook the clichés and hokum, finding in them a nobility of presence when what they actually embodied was a mind that, however, self-educated, had surrendered its real independence to a good deal of mystical rubbish.

2. See chapters 5 and 6 of Natalie Gittelson's *Dominus.* For an opposite view, see Michele Wallace's *Black Macho and the Myth of the Superwoman.*

3. Gittelson, *Dominus* (New York, 1978), p. 73.

4. For black writers, this is a no-win situation. Inevitably, their psyches will be dredged. "That Jones wrote with such fanaticism and hatred does not surprise me. First, Jones as an individual had to negate his former love affair with whites. Second, throughout the so-called calm period of his earlier poetry there repeatedly emerges the voice of a man who has a tremendous amount of anger bottled up inside of him." Michele Wallace, *Black Macho and the Myth of the Superwoman* (New York, 1978), p. 65.

Chapter Nine
Waiting

The American is a new man, who acts upon new principles; he must therefore entertain new ideas, and form new opinions.
—*de Crèvecoeur,* Letters from an American Farmer

I say we had best look our times and lands searchingly in the face, like a physician diagnosing some deep disease. Never was there, perhaps, more hollowness at heart than at present, and here in the United States. Genuine belief seems to have left us. The underlying principles of the States are not honestly believ'd in (for all this hectic glow, and those melodramatic screamings), nor is humanity itself believ'd in. What penetrating eye does not everywhere see through the mask? The spectacle is appalling. We live in an atmosphere of hypocrisy throughout. The men believe not in the women, nor the women in the men. A scornful superciliousness rules in literature. The aim of all the littérateurs *is to find something to make fun of. A lot of churches, sects, etc., the most dismal phantasms I know, usurp the names of religion. Conversation is a mass of badinage. From deceit in the spirit, the mother of all false deeds, the offspring is already incalculable.*
—*Whitman,* Democratic Vistas

I

WE GROW INTO THE VERY MYTHS we feed ourselves, as we aspire to believe that manhood is no longer necessary The new selves we yearn for loom before us like lost islands in the mind's storms. Behind us, the way it was; before us, the way it will be as soon as we can marry history to biology. Consciousness shatters and we suddenly see ourselves, stripped of the words that tell us how we *should* feel or what we *might* be. Alone, puzzled, the mind strains to discover that moment when the new man will be able to shed the old.

A man stands as the sole proprietor of his manhood. And yet, men today want so badly to surrender that ownership. We grow tired of the strains upon the self, of the need to examine others. Perhaps there is something to all this talk about the "fragility" of men, this speculation about the death of Eros, this grappling with sexual roles, this new balance which exists only in androgyny.

I find myself as split as every other man I know, irritated with all camps, dissatisfied with all definitions. On my desk, *Newsweek*'s cover offers me a smiling bespectacled man in a green and white checkered apron laboring over a stove who is looking down at his daughter playing near him. Inside, a predictable article, the sentences cloning into one another with a confusion that must be buried beneath clichés. "Men have always known it is a jungle out there from which few

breadwinners return intact." "Men are venturing to express
emotions once anathemetized as 'feminine.' " "The aggressive new challenge is shaking up a lot of men. In increasing
numbers, they are turning up at sex clinics and psychiatrists'
offices with worries about impotence or premature ejacula-
tion." The article reads like a computer printout designed to
translate those "tell me how you feel, how you *really* feel"
interviews into a common language of mutual approbation.
But it is not just men who are worrying in public about what
Newsweek headlines "How Men are Changing." On the other
side of my desk, an issue of *Ms.* offers "Secrets of the New
Male Sexuality." On the cover, the puzzled innocence of a
young man's face peers furtively from behind a craggy-faced
John Wayne mask. The tone of the articles inside blends
irritation with skepticism, implying that the changes desired
in American men will be too late and too superficial even if
they do come about.

How dead to the touch all this seems. We now need a
distancing between ourselves and the warfare we have waged
through our sexuality. Androgyny is a deceitful solution, a lie
we tell ourselves in order to catch hold of seemingly necessary
illusions. We decry "toughness"—that side of existence in
which the individual's need to survive thrusts against desperation—as being among the cardinal sins of men (and, by
implication, of women who insist on its powers). But toughness is neither virtue nor weakness, neither masculine nor
feminine; it is simply the will that gets one through each
crucial situation.

I want an end to all such categorical sexual definitions. In
making the importance of sexuality so overwhelming, we
have finally succeeded in making sex itself meaningless. For
sexuality itself now taxes not our capacities as men and
women but our very patience as human beings; for each of us,
it calls selfhood to the mark. *To be a man!* Necessity's inven-
tion, time's child. At eleven, I lie in the hospital room and

feel death like a passing presence, pausing at the foot of my bed. My father holds my hand. I wonder whether he can feel it, too. He tells me how, when he was eleven, he was taken by the Cossacks and forced to wander through Russia for two years. Today, the memory fills me with distance. It is not my body lying there, relinquishing the promise of an existence I could not yet understand. "Be brave!" commands my father. "Be a man!" In his own mind, he is wandering through the scarred Russian landscape. In the corner of the room, a friend of mine lies in an oxygen tent. He will die that night. Death is as personal as manhood, as courage. My father withdraws his hand from mine, and I close my eyes. In the morning, I wake up and both my father and the yellow oxygen tent are gone. Have I been brave? I wonder. Have I been a man?

And now I sit here at my desk, trying to frame all my remembrances and perceptions, new and old. I need a way to say it. I want the ambivalence that must live in each of us, but I want the solidity, too. Stretch the consciousness of any man or woman and we discover the need to re-create the self, as if each of us had been put on earth to rectify god's mistakes. I wonder whether I would be so much the prisoner of my inherited ideas about manhood if I were yet to triumph on that beach at Noordwijk, yet to rescue the self I wanted to create before that flickering moment of insanity took me. Would manhood then loom as the goal I made of it?

II

THE AGE DEMANDS! CRIED MAD EZRA. Certainly no age has demanded more of men than our own. The eroding presence, the passionate speeches linked to the less than passionate belief that there are still some possibilities left for manhood. The confusions of men have become the latest stimulus to conversation. We hear them discussed in bars, in elevators, at conferences of psychiatrists, at lunchtime gatherings of business executives. For most men, this has become *the* problem, one that embodies their relationships to women and to themselves.

I am the single man among six women in the elevator. As I follow them into the reception room, I notice that there is only one man for every five or six women. The conference is called "The Impact on Men of the Changing Role of Women." The women milling about seem a solid middle-class phalanx in the midst of a torn world. They seem to be enjoying themselves, their faces alive and buoyant. The men seem removed from the women and from each other; their faces are sculpted, frozen. I want to dismiss them, but I can sense my own discomfort and I cannot.

In the large lecture room I sit down on one of the molded plastic chairs. A young woman sits down next to me and takes pen and notebook from her bag. I suddenly remember that I, too, have come here to take notes and I remove a small notebook from my jacket pocket. I feel sheepish, out-of-place. A speaker steps up to the podium. When he mentions the "*maelstrom* of changing attitudes between men and women," he laughs, then bends over like a man in pain. From the audience, a woman's voice cries out, "*Peoplestrom!*" More laughter. I am even more uncomfortable.

The relationship between men and women in America, the speaker tells us, is a modern revolution. Men are losing battles because they refuse to shake off stereotypical roles. "How can you be brave enough to talk about how men feel when men do not talk about their feelings?" It seems to me that their feelings are all men *do* talk about today. But I listen attentively as the next man, a psychiatrist, takes the podium and begins his discussion of gender identity and fatherhood. Modern man, he tells us, is in retreat from woman; men, the

"fragile creatures," have become mere "experience collec-
tors." He wants a truce between the sexes. I nod. When he
concludes, a young woman in the audience asks a sharp-
edged question which I cannot hear but which is greeted by a
burst of applause from those near her. The hostility between
the two factions is extensive. Few of the women seem as
eager for a truce as the speaker.

Another psychiatrist follows—slender, gray-haired, a classic Arrow-shirt profile. He refers to his wife, a writer whose
work I have read and admire. I wish she were speaking. I
wish there were someone who might lend an honest voice to
all this sexual gerrymandering, someone who might touch
the human in each of us—man or woman—without this cloy-
ing jargon-ridden deadness. I hate a vocabulary which stuffs
each of us into his sexual assigned-risk plan.

He praises the woman's movement for its emphasis on
"relationships." He runs down the list of monsters which
have begun to rear their heads and tries to assure us that men
have never had it so good. Male sexual problems are not on
the rise; the myth of increased male impotence is simply not
true. The problems of men, he concludes, are simply "coming
out of the closet" in a society which now permits men to talk
about those problems.

The women in the audience applaud enthusiastically; the
men also applaud, but they turn to look at each other as they
do. I want to ask him whether there has ever been a time
when American men seemed to have less promise. It is too
simple to explain the problem away by denying it. Or by
repeating how each movement claiming its rightful due is
going to liberate its oppressor.

Of course, there is a need for men to transcend their past,
to get beyond the restrictions that manhood used to impose.
But give men something to affirm, too: The power in one's
self is a necessary reality. Why continue to insist upon the

unmitigated course of disasters that the struggle for manhood
has brought upon us? A catalogue of judgement as relentless
as the Book of Leviticus. Manhood is restrictive; manhood is
destructive to personality; manhood is brutal; unfeeling;
frightened; narcissistic; uncreative; fearful of its own inner
urgings; afraid of the unsettling voices that whisper to it;
bourgeois to the core; destructive to bourgeois solidity; indi-
vidualistic; conformist; competitive; timid; tyrannical; insen-
sitive; oblivious to the need for sexual transcendence;
removed from the powers of love, beauty, expression, body
language; manhood is success-oriented; manhood destroys
family life; it is too dependent upon family life; it is spiritually oblivious. Manhood is sexist! Gender is damnation! In
biology, we are guilty; in history, the record indicts us on our
own testimony.

As I leave the conference, the distinguished gray-haired
doctor is surrounded by a bevy of women and one hesitant
man who lingers at the rear of the group saying nothing.

I stop for a bourbon in a Chinese restaurant on the corner. I
would like nothing better than to get drunk. The relentless
cataloguing of gender has given me a headache. But I am a
man who walks on crutches and so I shrug my shoulders and
leave the restaurant. A man, after all, has certain responsibilities even with the accusatory finger levelled against him.

Another week, another conference. At the next one I at-
tend, a receptionist takes my name as I step off the elevator.
An older woman, with a 1950s blond coiffure, smiles me
inside and waves me over to the coffee bar where I am
handed "The *Playboy* Report on American Men," its cover
done in red, white, and blue with the omnipresent Playboy
Bunny in the center. There are more men than women here,
even three or four blacks. Still, it is a conference about the
problem.

On my right, two men are discussing the problem, and I

eavesdrop as I drink my coffee. One of them seems to be connected with the conference. The other is a thick fleshy man who nods continually while the first man speaks. "Not only do we have an obligation to our market, but we are probably the least-investigated group in all of America. We're *just* men. Christ, look at how many studies there've been of the attitudes of women over the past decade!" Like arguments from the early seventies that WASPs were the truly oppressed minority in America.

"My god, man, it's a revolution. All sorts of changes. Men using cologne, men wearing beards, mustaches, everything! In the fifties, a man wearing a wig would've been considered strange. A goddamn faggot. Now, 58% of men approve of hair transplants! Hair transplants! *Fifty-eight* percent, for Christ's sake!"

I finish my coffee and drift into the next room. A pollster begins to read from his report in a dull sociological monotone, a voice that tells you he is surprised at nothing, is willing to accept all human foibles from men or women or anything in between so long as they can be verified statistically. A black photographer, with four different cameras hanging from his shoulders, scours the auditorium for the best vantage points. He snaps one picture after another. I wonder what he thinks of the way in which manhood is now to be defined by market researchers. There is nothing to argue with in this report. Its "revolutionary" message is limited to the striking idea that men out there have a need for hairpieces and cologne. The *Playboy* Report insists that men want nothing more than "self-fulfillment and freedom to do one's own thing." As the monotone continues, I stare into space. The Report codifies the obvious.

III

WE ARE STILL LEFT WITH THE ISSUE of speaking to our sons. It
is an old issue, older even than the problem of manhood. For it
is not merely the beliefs of men that create their manhood but
rather those subtle ambitions that steal upon them unawares,
at night, in their dreams, moments which they hold to the
heart of their being and call their own. And our sons will read
all the reports and study all the statistics and still be left with
the oldest problem of all: How to be the man one sets out to
be. A man absorbs the times in which he lives, but he knows
that he can never liberate himself from those times, never
retreat into what was past. As we ourselves were condemned
to live in a time of change, so our sons will inherit that
change. In America, we learn to telescope the past even as we
rewrite it, root out a different idea of manhood for the future.
Perhaps that accounts for the fact that we are so susceptible
to the power of images, to the ease of manipulation. And
perhaps that is why we seem so uncertain about what can
legitimately be expected of a man   What would de
Crèvecoeur, so in love with the promise of the *new,* think if
he were able to walk the streets of our cities and search out
his "new man" in the alleys and corners of our desperation—
all the he-she bars, the stroker movies, all the junkies and the
pushers and all those totally bored even with the *new.* "What,
then, is the American, this new man?" What indeed?

Now we discover that we must search for manhood, that
very aspect of life our fathers and grandfathers could take for
granted. There are no models of endurance that our sons can
emulate; nor are there even models against whom they can
revolt or test themselves. The time is past when a man could
believe that he could fashion a self able to struggle with the

American world, and still function within the proscribed confines of manhood. The loss may be permanent. Like most of the men I know, I would like to believe that such a loss makes the culture and the man who exists in it all the richer. Deep down, however, I do not really believe that. None of us does. We are as afraid of the new world lying before us as we are hesitant about letting the old world go. The discoveries we have made may in fact serve us well in the future, but at present we are still wary of them. Men today are subject to pressures piling up from different directions; their confusion forces them to retreat into the self, to seek a way out of their fear of failure.

For we have discovered that the real issues facing men today are not really sexual at all. The real issues still have to do with courage, with the willingness to risk one's substance as a man, with the ability to capture that self one claims. If neither homosexuals nor blacks can restore to us that willingness to capture an independent selfhood, that should not prevent us from recognizing their willingness at least to take the risks. In our time, even parody in the service of manhood seems braver than what we possess.

And so we turn to all the sons still waiting on the beach. And we tell them that the legacy was always ambiguous. But to recognize that our idea of manhood must change is to create the paradox of its restoration. For it remains a serviceable idea, an attractive alternative to the mechanistic dead ends we see before us now. We must never permit ourselves to forget how costly the payment for manhood was—nor should we ever permit our sons to forget, for we would then be distorting both ourselves and history. And yet, as our sons gather on the beach to set off for new worlds, we should reach out to them, to tell them that it is not the metaphor of manhood they are condemned to live with but the condition. That may still be a fate worth trying, for them, for us, and for that Columbus who still lingers in each American man.

Bibliography

Aaron, Daniel. *The Unwritten War: American Writers and the Civil War.* New York: Knopf, 1973.

Adair, Nancy, and Adair, Casey. *Word is Out.* New York: Delta, 1978.

Alvarez, A. *The Savage God: A Study of Suicide.* New York: Bantam, 1971.

Anderson, Quentin. *The Imperial Self: An Essay in American Literary and Cultural History.* New York: Knopf, 1971.

Arieli, Yehoshua. *Individualism and Nationalism in American Ideology.* Cambridge: Harvard University Press, 1964.

Atkins, Thomas R., ed. *Sexuality in the Movies.* Bloomington, IN: Indiana University Press, 1975.

Baker, Carlos. *Ernest Hemingway: A Life Story.* New York: Scribner's, 1969.

Becker, Ernest. *The Denial of Death.* New York: Free Press, 1973.

———. *Escape from Evil.* New York: Macmillan, 1976.

Boorstin, Daniel J. *The Americans: The Colonial Experience.* New York: Vintage, 1958.

———. *The Americans: The National Experience.* New York: Vintage, 1965.

———. *The Americans: The Democratic Experience.* New York: Random House, 1973.

Brogan, D. W. *The American Character.* New York: Vintage, 1944.

Brown, Norman O. *Life Against Death: The Psychoanalytic Meaning of History.* Middletown, CT: Wesleyan University Press, 1959.

Chesler, Phyllis. *About Men.* New York: Simon & Schuster, 1978.

Cohen, Hennig, ed. *The American Culture.* Boston: Houghton Mifflin, 1968.

————. *The American Experience.* Boston: Houghton Mifflin, 1968.

Erikson, Erik H. *Childhood and Society,* rev. ed. New York: W.W. Norton, 1963.

Farber, Leslie. *The Ways of the Will: Essays Toward a Psychology and Psychopathology of the Will.* New York: Basic Books, 1965.

Farber, Manny. *Movies.* New York: Hillstone, 1971.

Farrell, Warren. *The Liberated Man.* New York: Bantam, 1975.

Feigen Fasteau, Marc. *The Male Machine.* New York: McGraw-Hill, 1974.

Fiedler, Leslie A. *Love and Death in the American Novel.* New York: Meridian, 1960.

Frederickson, George M. *The Inner Civil War: Northern Intellectuals and the Crisis of the Union.* New York: Harper Torchbooks, 1965.

Friedenberg, Edgar Z. *Coming of Age in America: Growth and Acquiescence.* New York: Vintage, 1965.

Frohock, W. M. *The Novel of Violence in America.* Boston: Beacon, 1964.

Gittelson, Natalie. *Dominus: A Woman Looks at Men's Lives.* New York: Farrar, Straus & Giroux, 1978.

Goffman, Erving. *Asylums: Essays on the Situations of Mental Patients and Other Inmates.* New York: Anchor, 1961.

——. *The Presentation of Self in Everyday Life.* New York: Anchor, 1959.

——. *Stigma: Notes on the Management of Spoiled Identity.* Englewood Cliffs, NJ: Prentice-Hall, 1963.

Goodman, Paul. *Growing Up Absurd.* New York: Vintage, 1962.

Gornick, Vivian, and Moran, Barbara K., eds. *Women in Sexist Society: Studies in Power and Powerlessness.* New York: New American Library, 1971.

Greer Germaine. *The Female Eunuch.* New York: Bantam, 1971.

Guttmann, Allen. *From Ritual to Romance: The Nature of Modern Sports.* New York: Columbia University Press, 1978.

Hardwick, Elizabeth. *Seduction and Betrayal: Women and Literature.* New York: Vintage, 1975.

Haskell, Molly. *From Reverence to Rape: The Treatment of Women in the Movies.* New York: Holt, Rinehart & Winston, 1974.

Hemingway, Gregory H. *Papa: A Personal Memoir.* Boston: Houghton Mifflin, 1976.

Hemingway, Mary Welsh. *How It Was.* New York: Knopf, 1976.

Huizinga, Johan. *Homo Ludens: A Study of the Play Element in Culture.* Boston: Beacon, 1955.

Isaacs, Neil. *Jock Culture, U.S.A.* New York: W.W. Norton, 1978.

Jones, Howard Mumford. *O Strange New World: American Culture, the Formative Years.* New York: Viking Compass, 1964.

——. *The Age of Energy: Varieties of American Experience, 1865–1915.* New York: Viking Compass, 1971.

Kammen, Michael. *People of Paradox: An Inquiry Concerning the Origin of American Civilization.* New York: Knopf, 1972.

Kaul, A. N. *The American Vision: Actual and Ideal Society in Nineteenth Century Fiction*. New Haven, CT: Yale University Press, 1963.

Kriegel, Leonard, ed. *The Myth of American Manhood*. New York: Dell, 1978.

Lasch, Christopher. *The New Radicalism in America, 1889–1963: The Intellectual as a Social Type*. New York: Vintage, 1965.

Levinson, Daniel J., with Darrow, Charlotte N., Klein, Edward B., Levinson, Marcia H., and McKee, Braxton. *The Seasons of a Man's Life*. New York: Knopf, 1978.

Lewis, R. W. B. *The American Adam: Innocence, Tragedy, and Tradition in the Nineteenth Century*. Chicago: Phoenix, 1955.

Martin, Jay. *Harvests of Change: American Literature, 1865–1914*. Englewood Cliffs, NJ: Prentice-Hall, 1967.

Mailer, Norman. *Advertisements for Myself*. New York: New American Library, 1959.

———. *Cannibals and Christians*. New York: Delta, 1966.

———. *Existential Errands*. Boston: Houghton Mifflin, 1972.

———. *Marilyn*. New York: Warner Paperback Library, 1973.

———. *The Presidential Papers*. New York: Bantam, 1963.

———. *The Prisoner of Sex*. New York: New American Library, 1971.

Marx, Leo. *The Machine in the Garden: Technology and the Pastoral Ideal in America*. New York: Oxford University Press, 1964.

Matthiessen, F. O. *American Renaissance: Art and Expression in the Age of Emerson and Whitman*. New York: Oxford University Press, 1941.

Millett, Kate. *Sexual Politics*. New York: Doubleday, 1970.

Mitchell, Juliet. *Psychoanalysis and Feminism: Freud, Reich, Laing and Women*. New York: Doubleday, 1974.

Novak, Michael. *The Joy of Sports: End Zones, Bases, Bas-*

kets, Balls, and the Consecration of the American Spirit. New York: Basic Books, 1977.

Parkes, Henry Bamford. *The American Experience.* New York: Vintage, 1959.

Rahv, Philip, ed. *Literature in America.* New York: Meridian Books, 1957.

Riesman, David, with Glazer, Nathan, and Denney, Reuel. *The Lonely Crowd: A Study of the Changing American Character,* rev. ed. New York: Anchor, 1956.

Robinson, W. R., ed. *Man and the Movies.* Baltimore, MD: Penguin, 1969.

Ross, Lillian. *Portrait of Hemingway.* New York: Simon & Schuster, 1964.

Roszak, Theodore. *The Making of a Counter-Culture.* New York: Anchor, 1969.

Ruitenbeek, Henry M. *The Individual and the Crowd: A Study of Identity in America.* New York: New American Library, 1970.

Schrag, Peter. *The Decline of the Wasp.* New York: Simon & Schuster, 1971.

Sexton, Patricia C. *The Feminized Male: Classrooms, White Collars, and the Decline in Manliness.* New York: Vintage, 1970.

Sheehy, Gail. *Passages: Predictable Crises of Adult Life.* New York: Dutton, 1976.

Sklar, Robert. *Movie-Made America: How the Movies Changed American Life.* New York: Random House, 1975.

Slater, Philip. *The Pursuit of Loneliness: American Culture at The Breaking Point.* Boston: Beacon, 1970.

Slotkin, Richard. *Regeneration Through Violence: The Mythology of the American Frontier.* Middletown, CT: Wesleyan University Press, 1973.

Smith, Henry Nash. *Virgin Land: The American West as Symbol and Myth.* New York: Vintage, 1957.

Sontag, Susan. *Illness as Metaphor.* New York: Farrar, Straus & Giroux, 1978.

Taylor, William R. *Cavalier and Yankee: The Old South and American National Character.* New York: Harper Torchbooks, 1961.

Teal, Donn. *The Gay Militants.* New York: Stein & Day, 1971.

Thompson, William Irwin. *At the Edge of History: Speculations on the Transformation of Culture.* New York: Harper, 1971.

Tripp, C. A. *The Homosexual Matrix.* New York: McGraw-Hill, 1975.

Wallace, Michele. *Black Macho and the Myth of the Superwoman.* New York: Dial, 1979.

Warner, W. Lloyd. *American Life: Dream and Reality.* Chicago: Chicago University Press, 1953.

Whyte, William Foote. *Street Corner Society.* Chicago: Chicago University Press, 1943.

Wilson, Edmund. *Patriotic Gore.* New York: Oxford University Press, 1962.

Wolfe, Don M. *The Image of Man in America.* Dallas: Southern Methodist University Press, 1957.

Wood, Michael. *America in the Movies.* New York: Basic Books, 1975.

Wright, Beatrice A. *Physical Disability: A Psychological Approach.* New York: Harper, 1960.

Yablonsky, Lewis. *The Extra-Sex Factor.* New York: Times Books, 1979.

Young, Philip. *Ernest Hemingway: A Reconsideration.* New York: Harcourt, Brace & World, 1966.

Ziff, Larzer. *The American 1890s: Life and Times of a Lost Generation.* New York: Viking Compass, 1968.